Table of Contents

License Agreement

This book (the "Book") is a product provided by HobbyPRESS (being referred to as "HobbyPRESS" in this document). You may not modify the Book or create any derivative work of the Book or its accompanying documentation. Derivative works include but are not limited to translations. You may not copy any part of the Book unless formal written authorization is obtained from us. HobbyPRESS will not be held liable for any advice or suggestions given in this book. If the reader wants to follow a suggestion, it is at his or her own discretion. Suggestions are only offered to help.

HobbyPRESS is an independent content developer NOT associated with nor endorsed by Bandai.

Preface

Welcome to the world of Gunpla. If you are holding this book, chances are you have recently built your first High Grade kit straight out of the box, or perhaps you are still staring at a sprue of colourful runners, wondering where to begin. You might have followed the instruction manual perfectly, snapping pieces together with a pair of basic nippers, only to look at the final result and feel something is missing. The robot looks like the one on the box, but it does not quite feel like the ones you see in magazines, online galleries, or on competition tables.

That feeling of wanting more from your model is exactly where this book begins.

For many newcomers, the leap from assembling a plastic robot to creating a miniature work of art seems impossibly wide. Terms like "seam line removal," "panel lining," "topcoating," and "weathering" sound less like modeling techniques and more like a foreign language. The sheer volume of tools, paints, and advanced kits available can be overwhelming, and the fear of ruining an expensive kit often stops beginners from trying anything beyond the most basic assembly. This book exists to close that gap.

Practical Gundam & Gunpla Modeling for Beginners is not a gallery of unattainable masterpieces. It is a workshop manual. It has been written with the assumption that you have never held an airbrush, you are unsure what sanding sponge to buy, and you might be building on a kitchen table with a limited budget. Every chapter is built around clear, repeatable processes that prioritise small, manageable steps over artistic leaps. You will learn how to improve your straight build before ever cutting a part for modification, and you will discover that professional-looking results come from mastering a handful of simple techniques, not from natural-born talent.

The other goal of this book is practicality. While many advanced modeling guides focus exclusively on customisation, painting, and diorama building, this book acknowledges that many Gunpla builders simply want a clean, sharp-looking model that stands proudly on a shelf. You will therefore find equal attention given to fundamental assembly skills —proper nub removal, sanding, applying decals, and protecting your work with a clear coat—as you will to more advanced topics like painting, panel scribing, and basic weathering.

Whether your dream is to build a perfectly out-of-the-box Master Grade with nothing more than a pair of nippers and a panel liner, or you aspire to create a fully painted, battle-weary diorama, the techniques in this book will serve as your foundation. Each chapter builds logically on the previous one, so you can work through the book sequentially or jump directly to the skill you need right now.

Above all, remember that Gunpla is freedom. The name itself is a contraction of "Gundam plastic model," but the spirit of the hobby is the opposite of rigid rules. There is no wrong way to build a kit, as long as you are learning and enjoying the process. This book simply provides a map of proven paths. Where you go from there is entirely up to you.

So gather your tools, clear your workspace, and choose a kit you are not afraid to learn on. Let us begin turning plastic parts into something you will be proud to call your own.

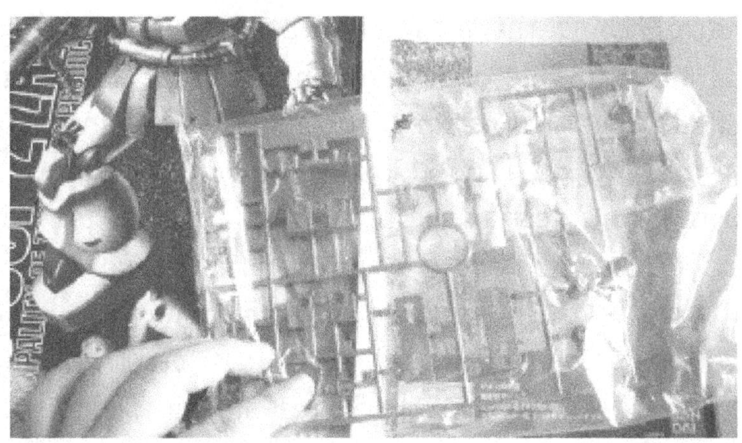

Introduction to Gundam mecha and Gunpla

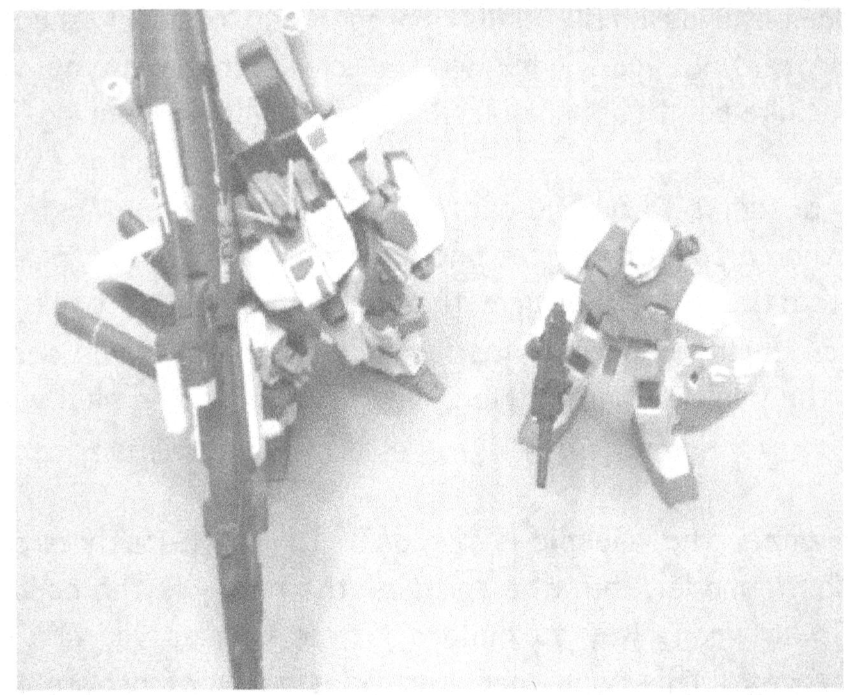

The core concept of a Gundam centers on a large bipedal vehicle controlled from a cockpit located in the torso, or "tummy," of the robot, with a camera built into the robotic head transmitting visual images to the pilot. Placing the cockpit in the torso is a deliberate design choice rooted in both practicality and dramatic tension. The torso is the largest, most stable volume of a humanoid machine, offering the most protection, while the head is relatively small and a prime target. This allows the head to function as an expendable sensor suite. Dramatically, this setup creates constant tension, as the head can be blown off leaving the pilot blind but alive, or the limbs can be severed turning the Gundam into a desperate last-stand artillery platform. The pilot is never truly safe. The head camera, or main sensor, is another brilliant realistic touch, feeding visuals to a 360-degree spherical monitor inside the cockpit, which has allowed pilots to see behind them or track multiple targets simultaneously, much like modern fighter jet sensor fusion but adapted to a humanoid frame.

Before Gundam's debut in 1979, giant robots were typically Super Robots—magical, almost invincible entities powered by willpower or mystical energy. Gundam changed everything by introducing realistic constraints. Its power source is rooted in Minovsky Physics, a fictional particle that allows for compact fusion reactors and beam weapons while also jamming radar, forcing combat to be visual and close-range. Weaponry includes projectile machine guns and bazookas alongside beam rifles, all subject to limited ammunition and power. The armor is a specific material called Lunar Titanium or Gundarium alloy, not an indestructible magical substance. The pilot is a soldier following orders and facing logistical concerns like fuel and repairs, not a hot-blooded hero who wins by yelling. Damage is cumulative and serious; a Gundam can run out of ammo or have its joints seized, which is a far cry from the cosmetic damage suffered by Super Robots. This single fictional leap of Minovsky Physics creates a logical basis for everything else, making giant humanoid mecha useful precisely because conventional radar is useless.

When Bandai released the first 1/144 scale Gundam model in 1980, it revolutionized plastic modeling. Before Gunpla, plastic models were mostly military vehicles or cars requiring glue and paint. Gunpla introduced snap-fit, multi-colored runners, allowing even a child to build a decent-looking robot in an hour with no additional tools. The hobby has since grown into three overlapping levels of engagement. The straight build is what most beginners do, simply assembling the model out of the box and applying sticker decals, and the fact that this yields a presentable model is a testament to Bandai's engineering. Painting and detailing is where the craft deepens, as hobbyists use airbrushes, panel-lining markers to accentuate recessed details, weathering powders to simulate battle damage, and custom decals to make a small plastic model look like an eighteen-meter-tall real machine. Customizing, or kaiso, is the advanced tier, including kitbashing or combining parts from multiple kits, scratch-building from raw plastic sheets, and full repaints into original color schemes, where the builder truly becomes a creator. Bandai has also created a tiered product line matching builder skill and desired realism, ranging from the simple and cheap Entry Grade and High Grade kits to the incredibly detailed Real Grade and Master Grade, culminating in the Perfect Grade kits that feature

LED units, moving armor hatches, and hundreds of parts for expert builders with deep pockets.

Underlying all of this is the deeper meaning that makes Gundam and Gunpla endure. The original series relentlessly shows the human cost of war, with the hero Gundam portrayed as merely a weapon and its pilot, Amuro Ray, a traumatized civilian teenager who suffers from post-traumatic stress disorder. The enemy faction, Zeon, is populated with sympathetic and noble characters, creating a moral ambiguity far removed from simple good versus evil. The hobby of building Gunpla serves as a direct thematic counterpoint to this anti-war message. Meticulously creating a model of a weapon of war becomes an act of patience, skill, and peaceful expression. The popular slogan "Gunpla is freedom" captures this idea perfectly, suggesting that there are no wrong ways to build and that the builder is not glorifying war but rather celebrating mechanical design, engineering precision, and creative craftsmanship. This combination of a consistent realistic logic, a tragic anti-war narrative, and an invitation to peaceful, meditative creativity through model building has made Gunpla a multi-billion-dollar phenomenon with over two thousand distinct kits and a thriving global community.

OOTB and OBB

Beyond the basic vocabulary of building and painting, the Gunpla community has developed its own specialized language to describe different approaches and techniques. Among the most fundamental of these terms are OOTB and OBB, which stand for Out Of The Box and Out of Box Build respectively. Despite the slight difference in wording, they both refer to exactly the same practice, which is more commonly known as a straight build. A straight build means assembling the model exactly as it comes from the manufacturer, using only the plastic parts included in the box and following the instruction manual without any modifications, custom painting, or aftermarket additions. You might still clip parts from the runners, snap them together, and apply the included sticker decals, but you would not sand down seams, fill gaps, or apply a custom color scheme. The remarkable engineering of modern Gunpla kits means that even a straight build can look quite impressive right out of the box, which is precisely where the name comes from. Many beginners start with OOTB builds, and even experienced builders will sometimes do a straight build for a kit they simply want to enjoy without the time investment of full customization.

Moving beyond straight building, the term kitbash describes a more creative and resourceful approach. Kitbashing means combining parts from different sources to create a single finished model. Those different sources might include multiple Gunpla kits of different grades or scales, parts from non-Gundam plastic model kits such as military vehicles or sci-fi ships, and even recycled parts from broken or incomplete builds. For example, a builder might take the torso and head from one Gundam kit, the arms and shoulders from another, the legs from a third, and then add thruster nozzles borrowed from a battleship model to create an entirely original mecha design. Kitbashing is especially popular among advanced hobbyists who enjoy designing custom mobile suits that Bandai has never officially produced. The appeal lies in the challenge of making disparate parts look like they belong together, which often requires cutting, reshaping, and gluing plastic, as well as extensive putty work to hide seams and gaps. The result is a truly one of a kind creation that exists only in the builder's imagination and on their workbench.

Scratchbuilding is slightly different from kitbashing, though the two techniques are often used together. To scratchbuild means to build a part for a kit entirely from scratch, using raw materials rather than repurposing existing pieces from other kits. The most common raw materials for scratchbuilding in Gunpla are sheets of polystyrene plastic in various thicknesses, commonly known as pla plate, along with plastic rods, tubes, beams, and putties. With these basic materials and a set of precision tools, a skilled builder can fabricate any part they can imagine, from a larger shoulder armor piece to an entirely new weapon or a detailed inner frame component that Bandai never included. Scratchbuilding is the most demanding technique in the hobby because it requires not only craftsmanship but also design skill, measurement precision, and the ability to visualize a three dimensional object from flat sheets of plastic. A builder might scratchbuild a part for any number of reasons, such as correcting a perceived flaw in the original kit, adding detail where the kit is lacking, repairing a lost or damaged piece, or creating something that has never existed in any kit. While kitbashing is about creative combination of existing elements, scratchbuilding is about pure creation from nothing, and the most impressive custom builds in competitions like the Gundam Builders World Cup often feature extensive scratchbuilt components that casual observers would mistake for original kit parts. Taken together, OOTB represents the hobby's accessible entry point, kitbash represents its spirit of creative reuse and combination, and scratchbuilding represents its highest expression of fabrication skill and design vision.

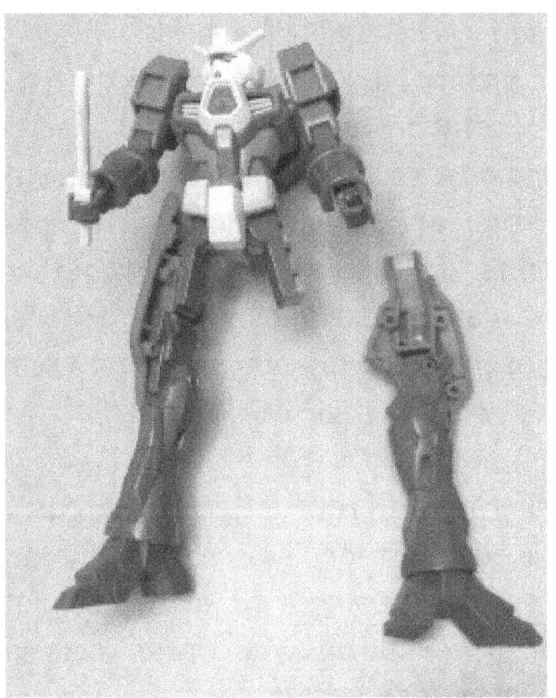

Gundam universes

Universal Century UC is the original Gundam universe that talks about wars between earth and its space colonies. Almost everything in all Gundam series has its roots in this universe (0079, 0080, 0083, Unicorn, Z, ZZ, F91 ...etc).

After Colony AC talks about colonies using Gundams to fight and achieve independence. Gundam Wing was the first AC story brought to the west by Cartoon Network).

Cosmic Era focuses on wars between genetically engineered humans living in space and normal humans living on earth. The famous Gundam SEED is the first Cosmic Era story.

After War AW took place near the end of a war between space colonies and Earth at the post-apocalyptic earth wasteland. It is mainly Gundam X in this universe. Future Century FC is all about the kung fu fight gundams. Anno Domini AD is all about some super human in the world of Gundam 00. There are many more, including the latest Gundam Age and Iron Blood Orphan. These universes do not always have any visible relationship with the UC.

Quality grading hierarchy

The quality grading hierarchy of Gundam models is organized into several distinct tiers, or grades, that help builders understand a kit's scale, complexity, part count, and level of detail before they begin. Each grade is designed for a different skill level and building experience, ranging from the most accessible and beginner-friendly kits to the most advanced and intricate engineering marvels.

Starting from the most accessible end of the spectrum, the Entry Grade, often abbreviated as EG, is a relatively recent addition to the lineup. These kits are built at 1/144 scale and are designed specifically for absolute beginners. They feature a very low part count, require no tools to remove parts from the runners, and offer a satisfying build experience at a very low price point, making them perfect for children or first-time builders. A related but older category is the First Grade or FG, also at 1/144 scale, which offers very simple and inexpensive kits with limited color separation and articulation, though this line has largely been succeeded by the Entry Grade in recent years.

The High Grade, or HG, is the most common and diverse line in the entire Gundam model ecosystem, serving as the standard for the hobby. At 1/144 scale, these kits offer a perfect balance of affordability, durability, and build complexity. While generally simpler than higher tier models, modern High Grade kits often feature surprising articulation and color separation, which makes them widely recommended as the ideal starting point for newcomers. Because the line covers almost every mobile suit from every Gundam series, it is also a favorite among experienced builders looking for a quick or custom project. A popular sub-line within this category is the High Grade Universal Century, or HGUC, which focuses specifically on mobile suits from the Universal Century timeline with a consistent level of quality and detail.

Stepping up in both scale and complexity, the Real Grade, or RG, also uses a 1/144 scale but packs an immense amount of detail into that small size. Introduced for the Gundam thirtieth anniversary in 2010, Real Grade kits feature a pre-molded inner frame and advanced color separation, effectively shrinking the complexity of a Master Grade kit into a High Grade sized package. Because of their small parts and intricate assembly, Real Grade kits are recommended for builders who have already completed several High Grade kits and are ready for a more challenging small-scale project.

When a builder is ready for a larger, more substantial build, the Master Grade, or MG, is the natural next step. At the larger 1/100 scale, these kits are a true cornerstone of the hobby. A defining feature of the Master Grade line is the fully articulated inner frame, which is assembled first and acts as a skeletal core for the model. This internal frame allows for superior poseability and realistic mechanical detailing. With part counts often exceeding five hundred pieces, a Master Grade kit is a significant project that results in a highly detailed, centerpiece-worthy display model. Within the Master Grade line exists a special sub-line called Ver. Ka, or Version Katoki, which consists of special releases designed by the renowned mechanical designer Hajime Katoki, known for their realistic proportions, distinctive decal sheets, and a high-detail aesthetic. For builders who like the 1/100 scale but want a less intensive build than a full Master Grade, the RE/100 line, which stands for Reborn-One Hundred, offers simplified internal structures with the same external scale and a focus on more obscure mobile suit designs that might not otherwise receive a modern kit.

At the absolute pinnacle of the hierarchy is the Perfect Grade, or PG. These are the largest mainstream kits available, built at a massive 1/60 scale. Perfect Grade kits are engineering marvels that represent the pinnacle of Gunpla design and manufacturing. They feature a full and incredibly detailed inner frame, often including working pistons, sliding armor panels that reveal the mechanics beneath, built-in LED lighting units, and even metal parts for structural integrity and weight. With part counts that can exceed one thousand pieces, Perfect Grade kits are long, complex, and expensive builds intended for expert modelers who want the ultimate building challenge and the most impressive possible display piece for their collection.

Beyond this main sequence from Entry Grade to Perfect Grade, there are several other distinct categories worth mentioning. SD, or Super Deformed, kits are a long-running line characterized by chibi proportions, giving familiar mobile suits large heads, small bodies, and a cute, cartoonish appearance. While generally simpler to build than their realistic counterparts, these kits are very popular for customization and fun. The Mega Size Model line is unique for its sheer scale at 1/48, making for very large and physically imposing models. However, these kits intentionally have a lower part count and simplified internal structure, focusing on size and presence over intricate internal detail. Finally, the term No Grade, or NG, is often used retroactively to refer to older kits from the nineteen eighties and nineteen nineties that were produced before the modern grading system was standardized. These kits vary wildly in quality and are often less detailed, requiring more work such as painting and seamline removal to look their best. Similarly, TV Series kits are models released alongside an anime series that do not fit neatly into the High Grade or other standard categories, and they vary in scale and quality, though they are often simpler in design than dedicated High Grade releases from the same era.

BAKUC and GWBC

BAKUC stands for the Bandai Action Kit Universal Cup, which was the official international Gunpla modeling competition organized by Bandai that ran from approximately 2003 until 2010, when it was rebranded and replaced by the Gundam Builders World Cup, or GBWC, starting in 2011. BAKUC actually evolved from an earlier competition called the Bandai Action Kit Asia Cup, or BAKAC, which began in 2003 and involved nine Asian countries including Malaysia, Japan, China, and Indonesia. As the popularity of Gunpla grew globally, Bandai expanded the competition in 2006 to include European countries such as Italy and the United States, and at that point the name was officially changed to BAKUC to reflect its new universal reach. By 2007, the competition had been opened to participants from Western nations including Italy, America, and Canada, and in 2010 Australia was added as well.

The structure of BAKUC involved regional qualifying rounds held in participating countries, with winners advancing to the World Finals held annually in Hong Kong around the end of the year, often as part of a larger Gundam Expo rather than as a completely standalone event. The competition was typically divided into categories based on age, such as an Open category for participants fifteen years and above and a Junior category for those under fourteen, with sometimes an additional OOB, or Out of Box, category for straight builds. The judging rules allowed for any type of modification, scratch building, remodeling, and diorama construction, though the use of commercial full resin or resin conversion kits was not permitted, and entries had to be made from original Bandai kits. All grades and scales were allowed.

One of the most memorable and beloved aspects of BAKUC was its mascot, a masked character known simply as Mr. BAKUC or the Masked BAKUC. First introduced by Bandai in 2006, this mysterious figure traveled freely around the world with the sole purpose of promoting Gunpla. He ate, slept, drank, and spoke only about Gunpla, and he could be found at every major Gunpla gathering and BAKUC event. His true identity, nationality, and origins remained a complete mystery, and his disappearance after the competition was rebranded is fondly remembered by longtime fans of the hobby. The 2009 finals were particularly significant because they coincided with the thirtieth anniversary of the first Gundam anime series, and in that year the Italian representative Francesco Coriglione achieved second place in the Open category, with Singapore taking first place and China taking third.

Ultimately, in 2011, Bandai decided to rebrand the competition, and BAKUC was officially renamed the Gundam Builders World Cup. With this change, the beloved masked mascot, Mr. BAKUC, was retired, much to the nostalgia of the Gunpla community. While the name BAKUC may no longer be in official use, it remains a significant part of Gunpla history, representing the first truly global effort by Bandai to unite modelers from Asia, Europe, and the Americas in a single, world-class competition, and the level of entries, particularly the massive dioramas, was noted to be very intense and had improved significantly year after year during its run.

GBWC stands for the Gundam Builders World Cup, which is the official, global level tournament for Gunpla building organized by Bandai Spirits. First launched in 2011, the GBWC is considered the ultimate competition for Gunpla enthusiasts, where participants from around the world compete to be crowned the world champion of Gunpla creation. The GBWC is a multi-stage event. Preliminary contests are held across sixteen different regions worldwide, including Japan, the United States, the United Kingdom, China, South Korea, Australia, and many others across Europe and Asia. Winners from each regional competition then advance to the World Finals, which are traditionally held at the Gundam Base in Tokyo, Japan. The competition is divided into age categories to ensure fair judging, typically a U Twenty course for participants under twenty years old and an Over Twenty One course for participants aged twenty one and older. Entries are judged based on a combination of three main criteria: craftsmanship, which covers building and assembly technique, painting and application, and creativity. Winners receive prestigious prizes, such as large scale, exclusive metallic busts of the iconic RX-78-2 Gundam. The search results also show that GBWC was used as the title for a spin-off pictorial novel series called Gundam Build Divers: GBWC, which stood for Gundam Build Divers: Jim and Ball's World Challenge, but this is a specific work of fiction based on the build fighter concept, not the real world competition. The official Bandai websites and all major news sources consistently use GBWC to refer to the world championship and make no mention of the term BAKUC in that context.

The Gunpla communities

As of the time of this writing, the most popular Gunpla groups span several platforms, each offering a different experience for builders of all skill levels. The largest and most active hub is the r/Gunpla subreddit on Reddit, which has grown to over three hundred thousand members and serves as the main online gathering place for the community. This group is known for its structured yet welcoming environment, featuring dedicated weekly threads like Work In Progress Wednesday and Finished Build Friday, as well as a bi-weekly Q&A thread where beginners can ask questions without feeling intimidated. The community shares honest reviews of new kits, detailed painting and panel lining guides, and noob-friendly advice, making it an excellent starting point for anyone new to the hobby.

For builders seeking more specialized knowledge, Gundam Model Builders, often abbreviated as GMB, is a dedicated forum that has existed for years and focuses on advanced techniques such as custom builds, scratch-building, resin casting, and professional-level weathering. Its gallery section is filled with impressive custom creations, and the active modding threads offer step-by-step tutorials for those looking to take their skills to the next level.

On Discord, real-time interaction thrives in several popular servers. The r/Gunpla official Discord offers a live chat space connected to the Reddit community, allowing for instant feedback and discussion. The GunplA Cafe server provides a relaxed atmosphere where members can show off builds, talk about collections, and meet fellow Gundam enthusiasts, with additional features like giveaways and community events. For those who prefer a more structured learning environment, the Gunpla Builder's Association, or GBA, Discord server has grown to over seven thousand six hundred members and emphasizes friendly, constructive feedback, knowledge sharing, and organized group builds and contests.

Facebook remains a valuable platform, particularly for regional and local groups, which are hidden gems for builders who want firsthand updates on limited edition kits available in their area, tips on local stores and shipping options, and opportunities to meet fellow builders at meetups. The Plastic Model Builders Group on Facebook, mentioned by veteran builders, has grown to approximately twenty six thousand members and serves as another significant gathering place.

For visual inspiration, Instagram is a treasure trove where hashtags like Gunpla and GundamModel bring together stunning photography, creative dioramas, and custom lighting setups from builders around the world. For those who prefer a portfolio-style platform, ModelSpace allows builders to document their progress using a builder's journal feature and showcase high-quality photos of their completed work.

Finally, for builders interested in more competitive or niche aspects of the hobby, there are specialized communities like r/advancedGunpla for those who want to go beyond out-of-box builds. The Mobile Suit Gundam Skirmish Discord server is unique in that it uses 1/144 scale Gunpla as figures for a fan-made tabletop wargame, and for builders following the competitive scene, GBWC remains the most prestigious global competition, with national qualifiers held in countries including Vietnam, China, Japan, and the United States. Each of these groups offers something different, and many builders participate in several at once to get the full range of community support and inspiration.

SOTSU and SUNRISE

To understand the world of Gundam modelling, it is essential to know the roles of two key companies, Sotsu and Sunrise, because while they are now both part of the same corporate family under Bandai Namco Holdings, they have historically played very different roles in bringing the Gundam universe to life.

Sunrise is the legendary animation studio responsible for the actual creation of the Gundam anime series and films. Founded in September 1972 by former employees of Mushi Production, the studio founded by Osamu Tezuka, Sunrise made a strategic decision early on to focus on the mecha genre, which was more difficult to animate but offered strong potential for toy sales. This gamble paid off spectacularly in 1979 when the studio produced the very first Mobile Suit Gundam series, directed by Yoshiyuki Tomino, which would go on to become one of the most popular and influential franchises in all of Japanese animation.

Over the decades, Sunrise has produced nearly every Gundam anime, including landmark series such as Zeta Gundam, Gundam Wing, Gundam SEED, and Gundam 00, as well as critically acclaimed non-Gundam works like Cowboy Bebop, Code Geass, Inuyasha, and Love Live. The studio is so renowned for the fluidity and quality of its animation that fans often refer to it as Sunrise Smooth. In 1994, Sunrise became a part of the Bandai Group, solidifying the link between the anime's production and the toy and model kits that would follow. More recently, on April 1, 2022, as part of a major corporate reorganization, Sunrise was restructured and its name was legally changed to Bandai Namco Filmworks Incorporated. Crucially, however, the famous Sunrise name has been preserved and is now used as a brand for the company's intellectual property production group, meaning it remains the creative heart that continues to produce new anime content.

Sotsu has a very different origin and function. Unlike Sunrise, Sotsu is not an animation studio but rather a company specializing in advertising, marketing, planning, and most importantly, copyright management and licensing. Sotsu was originally founded in October 1965 as the Toyo Agency, a company that managed licensing for the Yomiuri Giants baseball team. In 1972, it produced its first television program, Thunder Mask, and entered the character licensing business. Sotsu's most significant move came in 1979 when it acted as a producer and funding partner for the original Mobile Suit Gundam television series. Crucially, Sotsu retained a significant share of the intellectual property rights to the franchise. This established a long-standing partnership where Sunrise would create the content and Sotsu would manage the business of licensing that content out for merchandise, toys, video games, and other products worldwide. This arrangement led to overlapping operations, but in 2019, Bandai Namco Holdings moved to consolidate its control by acquiring Sotsu through a tender offer, making it a wholly owned subsidiary, which brought the full licensing power of the Gundam intellectual property under one roof.

Today, the relationship between Sotsu and Sunrise, now Bandai Namco Filmworks, is being streamlined to make the management of the Gundam franchise more efficient, especially as Bandai prepares for major international projects like a live-action Gundam film in partnership with Legendary Pictures. Under a planned restructuring set to take effect on April 1, 2026, Bandai Namco Filmworks will consolidate its hold on the Gundam business, handling the planning, production, and copyrights, while Sotsu will focus specifically on commercialization in Japan and overseas.

The most popular scale

The most popular scale for Gunpla is overwhelmingly 1/144, largely because it is the standard scale for the High Grade line, which is the most accessible and widely available category of kits. Following that are 1/100, used for Master Grade and some larger High Grade kits, and 1/60, used for the premium Perfect Grade line.

What makes High Grade kits special is that they are the heart of the hobby for several key reasons, as they are specifically designed to balance quality, affordability, and ease of assembly, making them the perfect starting point for new builders. At 1/144 scale, completed kits stand approximately thirteen centimeters, or roughly five inches, tall. This smaller size keeps the amount of plastic low, meaning prices typically range from fifteen to thirty US dollars, and the kits also take up less space on a display shelf. High Grade kits use snap-fit assembly, which means no glue is required, and many parts are also color molded, allowing the model to look very close to its anime appearance straight out of the box without needing paint. Furthermore, the engineering in modern High Grade kits has advanced significantly, offering excellent articulation and color separation that rivals much more expensive kits from just a few years ago, so the entry-level label should not be mistaken for low quality.

While a larger box often contains a larger model, the grade of the kit is a much more reliable indicator of a kit's complexity and detail than the physical box size. A 1/144 Real Grade kit actually has a higher part count and complexity than a 1/100 High Grade kit, even though the Real Grade is physically smaller. The box size usually reflects the number of runners, or parts, inside, which correlates to complexity, not just the final height of the model. As a general rule of thumb, the scale tells you the final size while the grade tells you the building experience. 1/144 scale kits, including High Grade and Real Grade, are roughly palm-sized and represent the standard size. 1/100 scale kits, including Master Grade and Full Mechanics, are larger at roughly the size of a tablet or a thick novel. Finally, 1/60 scale Perfect Grade kits are the pinnacle, standing about a foot or thirty centimeters tall.

The first generation 1:144 kit released in the 80s.

The 1:144 Gundam AGE Advanced Grade AG beginner kits are very easy to assemble – the joints are fixed so there is not much flexibility. The manual is printed in the box with no separate manual. You do not need to use any glue to glue the parts – assembly is fairly easy for junior model builders. Since all the parts are already colored, there is no further need to paint the models.

The High Grade HG Series features poly caps for the joints, individual molded colors (ideal for those who hate to do painting by hand), as well as a modular construction similar to the 1/100 scale series. Simply put, the HGs have better colors, finer details and more flexible joints out of the box.

The 1:144 HG kit.

The primary difference between higher grade products and their lower grade counterparts is the joint design, which directly relates to how posable the finished products are.

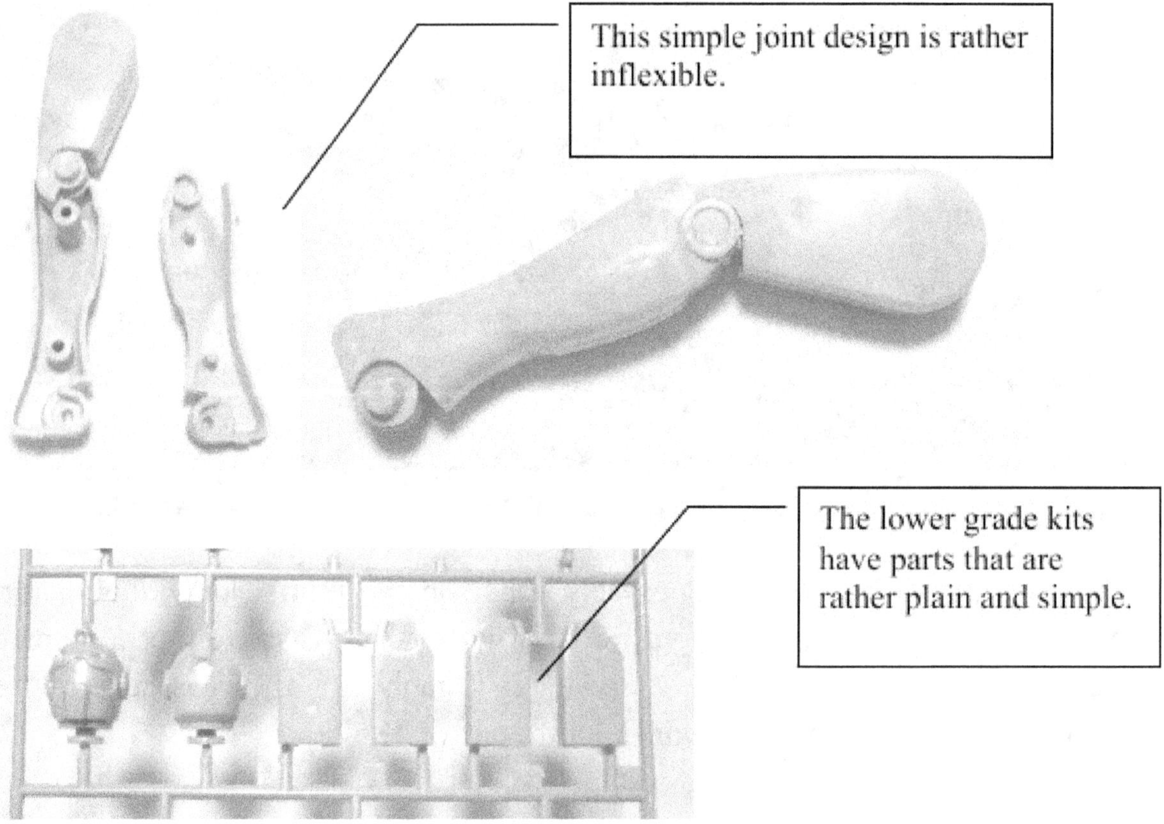

This simple joint design is rather inflexible.

The lower grade kits have parts that are rather plain and simple.

The SD series are the special cutie version of Gundam models. They are more for fun than for series modeling. Definitely not my cup of tea........

The Mega Gundam series are very large scale (1:48) Gundam model kits. They are VERY expensive.

UCHG

The U.C. Hard Graph series, often abbreviated as UCHG, is a unique and highly specialized line of Gunpla kits from Bandai that stands apart from the vast majority of Gundam models. While most kits focus on the giant humanoid mobile suits themselves, the U.C. Hard Graph series is dedicated to everything else in the Universal Century timeline, meaning the vehicles, support equipment, and the soldiers who crew them.

The most defining feature of the U.C. Hard Graph series is its scale and construction philosophy, as the main line of kits is built at a large 1/35 scale. To put that in perspective, this makes them significantly larger than the standard 1/144 scale of most High Grade kits and even bigger than the 1/100 Master Grade line. However, the scale is only part of the story, because the series is explicitly designed as a hybrid, blending the snap-fit assembly and pre-colored plastic of a typical Gunpla with the extreme mechanical detail and realistic finish of a military model. This focus on realism earned it the Hard Graph name, which refers to a highly detailed, hard technical schematic, and these kits are not about dynamic poses but about capturing the authentic feel of military hardware.

The core concept of the U.C. Hard Graph series is to expand the Real Robot genre by focusing on the mundane but essential elements of a mechanized army, giving modelers the chance to build the support structures that make the mobile suits possible. The catalog includes a diverse range of items, such as the Zeon Mobile Scout Set, which features a small hover vehicle known as the Wappa along with two pilots, the Ramba Ral Commando Set featuring the iconic Zeon ace, his motorcycle, and his troops, the 61st Type 5 Tank Semovente, and the centerpiece FF-X7 Core Fighter from the original RX-78-2 Gundam. These kits almost always come with highly detailed 1/35 scale figures of pilots, officers, and mechanics, as well as realistic accessories like toolbags, rifles, rations, and diorama bases including tables and chairs, allowing builders to create incredibly realistic slice-of-life dioramas from the One Year War rather than just a solitary robot on a stand.

The building experience of U.C. Hard Graph kits is accordingly more demanding than standard Gunpla. While many Gunpla kits are designed for a quick, glue-less snap fit, the U.C. Hard Graph series requires more from the builder. The construction is more involved, and while some parts are snap-fit, many pieces are designed to be cemented together, similar to a traditional model tank or aircraft. The level of detail is extremely high, featuring intricate panel lines and mechanical interiors such as a fully detailed cockpit in the Core Fighter kit. While parts are typically pre-colored, painting and weathering are highly encouraged to bring out the full military realism the kits are known for, which means the series is generally recommended for experienced modelers who are comfortable with advanced techniques.

The popularity of the concept led to the creation of spin-off manga and novels, also titled U.C. Hard Graph, which explored the lives of ordinary soldiers and mechanics during the One Year War. Furthermore, the series also has a sub-line called HG U.C. Hard Graph, or HGUCHG, which are not 1/35 scale kits but rather expansion sets for the standard 1/144 High Grade Universal Century kits. For example, a Zaku Ground War Set would include a standard 1/144 Zaku II kit alongside new runners for 1/144 scale support vehicles like the Wappa and the 61st Tank, plus small-scale figures, allowing builders to enhance their standard HGUC displays with the same military realism and diorama potential.

HGM and HY2M

Both HGM and HY2M refer to specialized, and now mostly discontinued, lines of model kits from Bandai that stand apart from the mainstay grades like High Grade or Master Grade. The High Grade Mechanics line, abbreviated as HGM, is a very niche series that focuses exclusively on the massive Mobile Armors from the Mobile Suit Gundam 0083: Stardust Memory OVA series. What makes these kits unique is their scale, as they are produced in 1/550 scale, which is tiny compared to a standard High Grade kit, because the Mobile Armors they represent are enormous in the anime. For example, the Dendrobium and the Neue Ziel, two of the most iconic units in this line, are so large that even at this small scale they are display worthy. The line was very limited, releasing only three kits between 2001 and 2002, and they are notable for including small figurines of the smaller mobile suits to complete the diorama. Because of their age and niche focus, HGM kits are considered collector's items today.

The Hyper Hybrid Model line, or HY2M, is a far more ambitious and diverse series that is best understood as Bandai's premium showpiece line focused on lighting and sheer size. The Hyper Hybrid name refers to the blend of a large scale plastic model with electronic gimmicks, primarily LED lights embedded in the head and thrusters. The line is most famous for its absolutely stunning 1/12 scale kits of the RX-78-2 Gundam and Char's Zaku II, which stand approximately 150 centimeters, or about five feet, tall, making them the largest official Gunpla kits ever produced. These massive models feature lights, sounds, and weapons that, due to their scale, can actually be used for cosplay. The price for these kits is extremely high, with the Gundam retailing for around three hundred and fifty thousand yen, or over thirty five hundred US dollars, and some limited edition versions selling for much more on the secondary market. Beyond these human sized centerpieces, the HY2M line also included the HY2M Glorious series, which consisted of 1/60 scale kits featuring extensive LED lighting, and a unique set of add-on parts for the standard 1/100 Master Grade line. These Master Grade upgrade kits were sold separately and contained replacement head parts with built in LED units and magnetic switches for popular mobile suits like the Zaku II and the Gundam, allowing modelers to add a light up feature to their existing Master Grade kits without complex wiring. Both the HGM and HY2M lines are now discontinued, so new kits are not being produced, and they primarily appear on the secondary market through auction sites and specialty retailers.

MG kits for beginners

For someone who has never built a plastic model kit before, starting with an MG presents several challenges that could be frustrating or overwhelming. An average High Grade kit might have one hundred to two hundred parts, whereas a modern Master Grade kit can easily have four hundred to six hundred or more parts, meaning the build time is significantly longer, often eight to fifteen hours or more compared to a two to four hour HG build, which requires a level of patience and sustained focus that a newcomer may not have developed yet. The defining feature of most MGs is the fully articulated inner frame, which the builder assembles first as a complex sub-assembly of dozens of pistons, pipes, and joints before any armor goes on, and understanding how these parts fit and move can be daunting for a first build. Furthermore, MGs are known for their high levels of detail, which often comes in the form of very small pieces for verniers, sensors, and panel accents that can be easy to lose, break, or misplace for a beginner not accustomed to handling delicate plastic parts. The cost is also a factor, as an HG kit typically costs fifteen to thirty US dollars while an MG kit usually ranges from forty to eighty dollars, with larger or more elaborate MGs costing over one hundred dollars, making mistakes on an expensive kit more painful and creating pressure that can take the fun out of learning. Finally, the plastic runners or frames for MGs often have more and smaller connection points called gates that require more careful removal with proper tools to avoid damaging the part, whereas an HG is much more forgiving of less than perfect nipper work.

Despite these points, some beginners do successfully start with an MG, and this is often the case for someone who is not a beginner to all modeling but rather a beginner specifically to Gunpla. If a person has previous experience building model cars, military aircraft, or tanks, which often require glue and paint, an MG Gunpla kit with its snap-fit assembly and pre-colored parts will feel surprisingly straightforward and well engineered. A very careful, patient, and detail oriented individual who is a huge fan of a specific mobile suit can absolutely succeed with an MG as long as they go slowly, follow the manual closely, and invest in the right basic tools such as good nippers, tweezers, and a file or sanding stick. Additionally, some older Master Grade kits, sometimes called No-Grade or early MGs from the nineteen nineties and early two thousands, are significantly simpler, such as the MG Gundam Ver. 1.5 or the MG Zaku II Ver. 2.0, which are less complex than modern MGs like the MG Barbatos or MG Freedom 2.0, though recommending these requires specific knowledge.

One might think that the smaller 1/144 scale Real Grade would be the intermediate step between HG and MG, but it is not, because RG kits are arguably even less suitable for beginners than MGs. They pack a Master Grade level of parts, often three hundred to four hundred or more, and an intricate pre-molded inner frame into a tiny High Grade sized body, making the parts minuscule and fragile, so RG is almost universally recommended as an advanced grade for builders with several HG or MG kits under their belt.

For a true first time model builder, a High Grade kit is almost always the best starting point because it provides the fundamental experience of building a Gunpla with very low risk of frustration, cost, or time commitment, and finishing an HG successfully builds confidence and skills that directly translate to an MG. However, for a motivated beginner who has some modeling experience or a very careful disposition, an MG is not impossible, and a good first MG would be a relatively modern, well regarded, and not overly complex kit such as the MG Gundam 2.0 or 3.0, the MG Jegan, or the MG GM Sniper II, all of which are known for solid, enjoyable builds that are more about the experience than fragility. In short, HG is for learning to walk while MG is for learning to run, and while you can skip walking, it is a much bumpier ride, so the vast majority of experienced builders will tell you they are glad they started with a few HGs before tackling their first Master Grade.

Using putty on HG and MG kits

The question of whether there is no need to use putty on HG and MG kits is a common one, and the short answer is that it is not strictly true that putty is never needed, though the reasons and frequency differ greatly between the two grades. To clarify, it helps to distinguish between two different modeling needs: the need for glue and the need for putty.

For all modern Gunpla kits, including both HG and MG, glue is almost never required for assembly because the kits are designed with a snap-fit system where parts are held together by friction and precise engineering, allowing a builder to complete the entire model using only their hands or basic nippers. Putty, however, serves a completely different purpose. It is not for holding parts together but rather for filling gaps and hiding seam lines, which are the visible lines that appear where two halves of a part, such as a forearm or a leg, are joined together. This is where the major difference between HG and MG kits becomes apparent.

Master Grade kits are engineered to a higher standard of part separation, meaning that seam lines are often cleverly disguised as panel lines or armor joints, or they are placed in locations where they are not visible on the completed model. Therefore, for most MG kits, a builder can achieve a fantastic result without ever touching a tube of putty because the advanced engineering does the work for them.

High Grade kits, on the other hand, are designed primarily for affordability and ease of assembly rather than for hiding every single seam. As a result, seam lines are frequently more noticeable and located on prominent areas like the arms, legs, and weapons. A builder can certainly assemble an HG kit without putty and it will look good, especially for a straight build. However, for those who want a more finished or realistic look, moving beyond a simple snap-build to achieve a competition-grade finish, using putty or plastic cement to eliminate these visible seams is a common and often necessary step.

Contents of a typical Gundam model kit and minimum age requirement

When you open a standard Gunpla kit, you will find several types of items inside the box. The most obvious are the plastic runners, which are the large frames containing all the plastic pieces of the model still attached to a plastic skeleton, and a typical High Grade kit might have five to ten runners while a more complex Perfect Grade kit can contain over fifty. The kit also includes foil and marking stickers, which are used to add color details such as eyes or sensors as well as official emblems and warning markings to the model, though more detailed kits often include dry-transfer or waterslide decals for a more professional finish.

The instruction manual is another essential component, presented as a comic style booklet that guides the builder step by step through the assembly process with clear diagrams, and it often features technical illustrations and background lore about the mobile suit. Depending on the kit, there may also be optional special parts such as pre-assembled inner frames, which are common in Real Grade and Master Grade kits, LED units for lighting up the eyes or thrusters, or interchangeable hands and weapon parts.

Most standard Gunpla kits do not include an Action Base display stand because they are designed to stand on their own two feet. However, there are frequent exceptions, as Action Bases are usually sold separately, allowing the builder to purchase one only if they want to display their model in a dynamic in-flight pose. Additionally, some special edition kits, such as Option Parts Sets, or larger more expensive models like Perfect Grades, will sometimes include a custom display base or adapter.

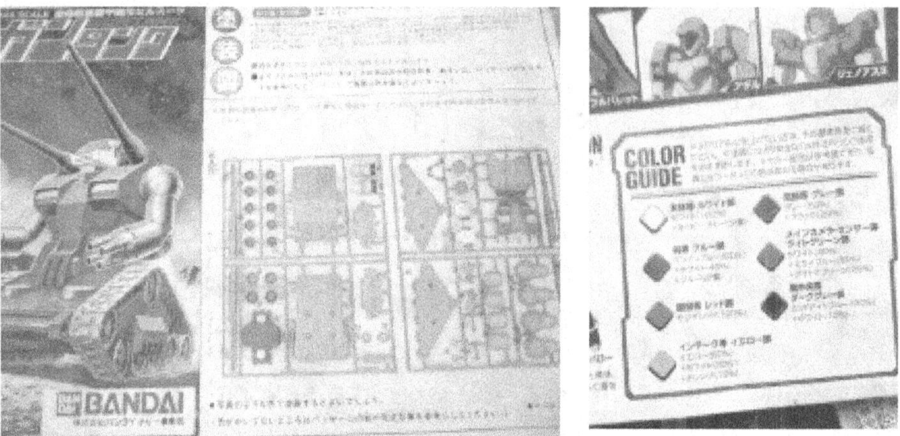

The minimum age requirement for Gunpla varies significantly based on the complexity and part size of the kit, but there is a strict safety warning regarding small children. All official Bandai Gunpla kits carry a warning that they are not suitable for children under three years of age due to the choking hazard posed by small parts. Most standard kits, including High Grade and Real Grade, are officially recommended for modelers aged eight and up, though retailers often note that due to the complexity and small parts, a kit is generally suitable for older children. The more advanced categories, such as Real Grade and Master Grade, are frequently recommended for ages fifteen and older because of their higher part counts, smaller pieces, and the greater patience required for assembly.

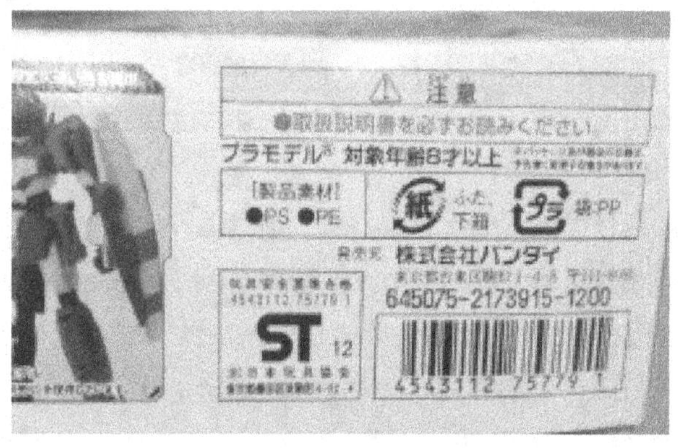

    HobbyPRESS.net (Hong Kong).

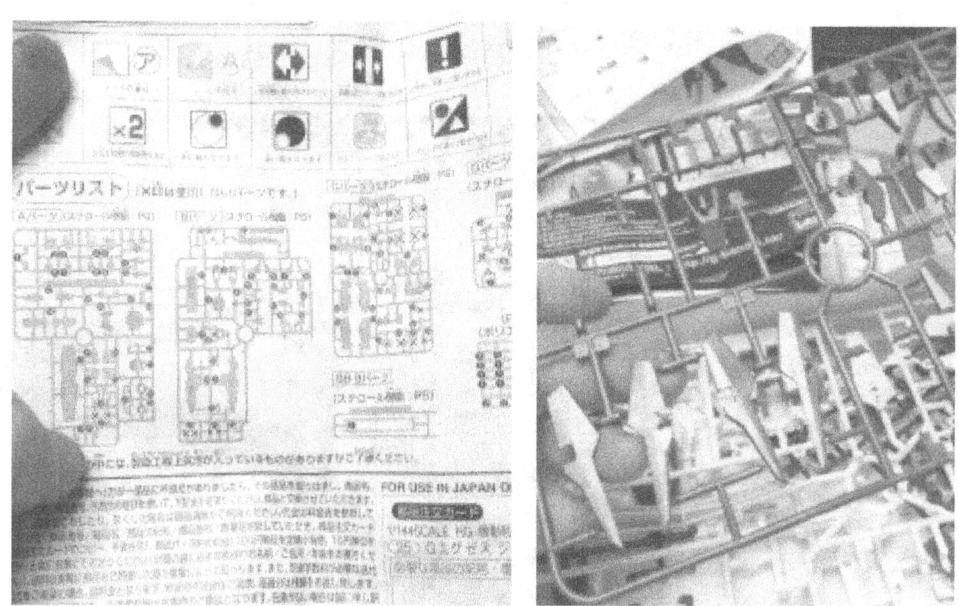

The first thing to do after opening up the box is to inspect everything and make sure nothing is missing from the kit. The manual clearly lists all the parts so it would be very easy for you to perform visual inspection.

Most Gundam model kits have NO stand included, with a few exceptions.

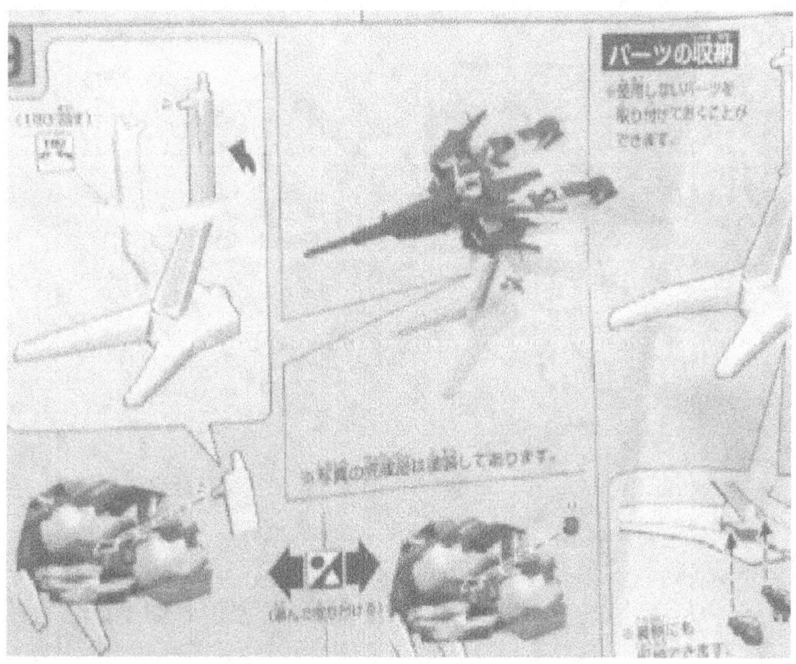

BTW, you can purchase the Action Base stand separately.

These stands are not expensive at all.

The Action Base stand has cool mechanical detailing and panel lines. There are holes for placing the support pole for the main stand to adjust the height. Both 1/144 and 1/100 models can be supported. Assembly is required.

Diorama set for Gundam

Long time ago, yes. The kits (only for the 0079 series) have been re-released recently.

The most prominent and modern line of official diorama products is the Realistic Model Series, or RMS, manufactured by MegaHouse, which is specifically designed for use with 1/144 scale kits, particularly the popular High Grade line. The RMS products fall into a few distinct categories depending on the type of scene one wants to create. One of the most spectacular options is the Catapult Deck series, which recreates the launch bay of famous carrier ships from the anime. These are large, premium display pieces that turn a shelf into a mobile suit hangar. For instance, there is a diorama of the Nahel Argama's catapult deck that measures approximately one hundred centimeters, or about thirty nine inches, in length, providing ample space to display multiple Gunpla in a launch sequence. A version based on the Argama from Zeta Gundam has also been released, which even includes seven small character figures to populate the deck and make the scene more lively.

Another major branch of the Realistic Model Series is the G Structure or G

Diorama Model line. While the Catapult Deck focuses on ship interiors, the G Structure line aims to recreate specific, iconic locations or moments from the Gundam universe. For example, there is a diorama of the MS Hangar from Mobile Suit Gundam: The Witch from Mercury, which is the storage container used for the show's duel scenes. This particular kit features moving parts like sliding hatches and rotating bases, and it includes water-slide decals for added detail. The G Structure line also recreates famous battlefields and environments, with sets including Jaburo's Fall, depicting the underground Federation base under Zeon attack, and New Yark City Ruins, showing a devastated urban landscape from Mobile Suit Gundam Hathaway. For fans of Gundam SEED, there is even a diorama of the Archangel's bridge.

Beyond these large scale sets, smaller and more affordable diorama accessories are also available. The G Structure Tragedy Diorama series offers compact scene kits that recreate specific dramatic moments from various episodes, with a height of about sixteen centimeters. For builders who enjoy creating their own unique landscapes, third party companies offer generic diorama building supplies such as foliage, grass tufts, and terrain elements, which can be used to customize any display.

It is important to note that these diorama sets are almost always sold separately from the Gunpla models themselves. While the Realistic Model Series line is explicitly designed to be compatible with 1/144 scale kits, the model kit is not included, and the builder will need to provide their own Gundam to place in the scene. Even with that in mind, for any dedicated Gunpla builder, these diorama sets offer a fantastic way to elevate a collection from a simple row of models to a series of dynamic, storytelling displays.

The U.C. Hard Graph series from Bandai is also explicitly designed for diorama creation, though its approach is quite different from the pre-built, scene in a box diorama sets described earlier. While the Realistic Model Series from MegaHouse provides complete, pre-designed display bases like catapult decks or hangar interiors, the U.C. Hard Graph series takes a more fundamental approach to diorama building by offering the highly detailed building blocks that modelers use to construct their own custom dioramas from the ground up.

The U.C. Hard Graph series, launched by Bandai in September 2006, is unique because it deliberately moves away from focusing on giant mobile suits themselves and instead concentrates on the human-scale elements of the Universal Century battlefield. The series features 1/35 scale kits of support vehicles like the Zeon Wappa hover scout and the M61A5 main battle tank, as well as detailed soldier figures, weapons, and even partial mecha components such as a Zaku II head or the forearm of a fallen Gundam. This focus on smaller, realistic elements is specifically intended to allow builders to create dynamic and realistic dioramas that depict the everyday aspects of the One Year War, such as a mobile suit launch preparation or an anti-MS squad setting up a rocket launcher.

The term Hard Graph itself refers to a highly detailed technical schematic, and this is reflected in the kits' design philosophy. They blend the snap-fit, multi-colored plastic tradition of Gunpla with the extreme mechanical detail and realistic finish expected from traditional military scale models. While some parts are snap-fit, many pieces are designed to be cemented together, and painting and weathering are highly encouraged to bring out the full military realism that makes these kits shine in a diorama setting. It is worth noting that the U.C. Hard Graph branding also appears in a sub-line called HG U.C. Hard Graph. These are not the large 1/35 scale kits but rather expansion sets for the standard 1/144 High Grade Universal Century line. These sets, like the Zaku Ground War Set, include a standard 1/144 mobile suit alongside new runners for 1/144 scale support vehicles and small figures, allowing builders to enhance their standard HGUC displays with the same diorama-focused philosophy. In summary, the U.C. Hard Graph series is indeed a diorama-oriented product line, but it is a builder's diorama series. Instead of providing a complete, pre-designed scene, it supplies the highly realistic vehicles, figures, and mechanical parts that give advanced modelers the raw materials to design, customize, and build their own unique and detailed dioramas from scratch.

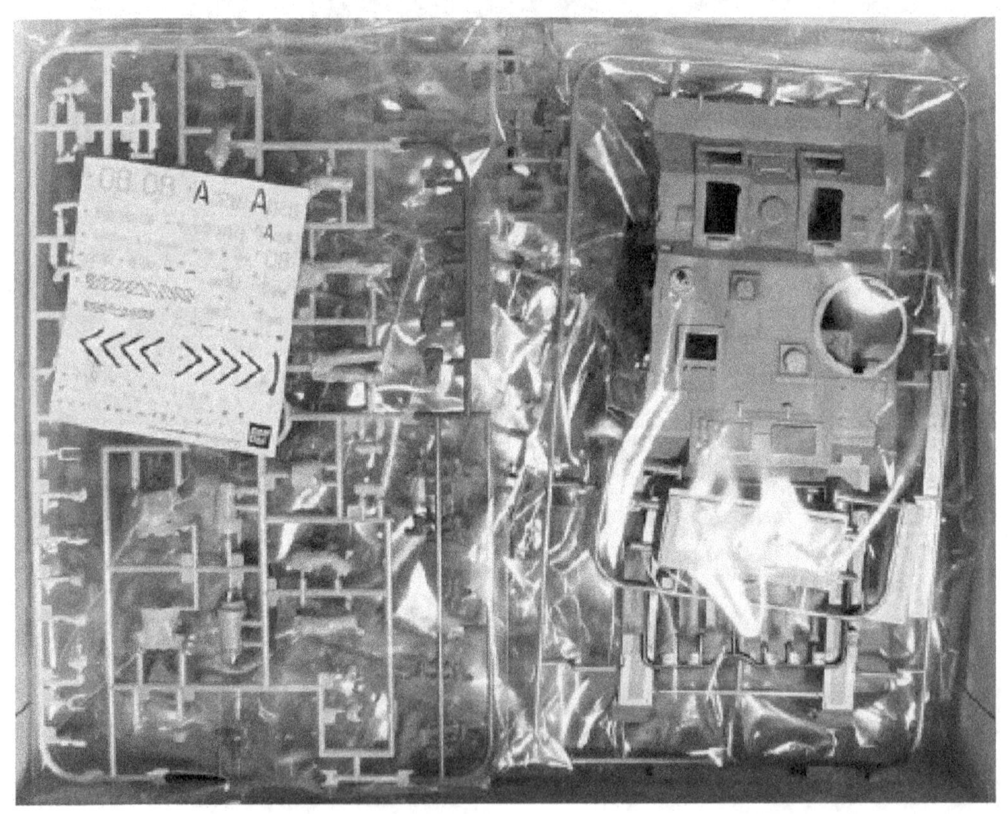

Ver. Ka models and Robot Spirits

The Ver. Ka designation is one of the most highly regarded labels in the Master Grade lineup, representing a distinct vision for Gunpla rather than just a simple variant or color swap, as the "Ka" stands for "Version Katoki," referring to the renowned mechanical designer Hajime Katoki, who began reimagining iconic mobile suits under his own personal label starting in 2002. What makes these kits special is that each Ver. Ka is a complete redesign from the ground up, not a minor tweak or an accessory pack, and it brings Katoki's distinctive design philosophy to every release.

The aesthetic of a Ver. Ka kit is immediately recognizable and fundamentally different from standard Master Grade offerings because while typical MG kits aim for faithful anime accuracy, reproducing the mobile suit exactly as it appeared on screen, Ver. Ka takes a different approach by leaning toward a sharper, more precise, almost industrial mechanical style. Katoki is known for refining and modernizing proportions, giving his designs slender limbs, smaller heads, and a distinctive short thigh with long lower leg proportion that creates a sleek, heroic silhouette. The panel lines are crisper and more technical, and the mechanical detail is denser, with vents, hatches, thrusters, and surface textures that suggest a machine designed for actual battlefield deployment. The iconic Katoki stance, with feet planted shoulder-width apart, elbows slightly bent, and standing tall and straight, has become synonymous with his design presentations and is featured prominently on Ver. Ka packaging, which often uses a distinctive clean white background rather than the traditional action-oriented box art.

Perhaps the most defining and notorious feature of Ver. Ka kits is the decal work, as every Ver. Ka kit comes loaded with premium waterslide decals rather than the foil stickers or dry transfers found in most standard Gunpla releases. These sheets are packed with an immense number of unit markings, caution labels, serial numbers, maintenance warnings, faction insignias, and technical specifications that can cover almost the entire surface of the kit. The quantity of decals has become legendary among builders; for example, the MG Sinanju Ver. Ka includes 268 dry decals and reportedly took one builder fifteen hours just to apply them, while the MG Psycho Zaku Ver. Ka includes a decal sheet large enough to cover a person's face. When applied carefully, these decals transform the finished build into something that looks like it was pulled straight out of a military hangar or engineering bay, though the application process is time-consuming and requires significant patience. Some builders criticize this over-decaling as excessive, but for many enthusiasts, the decal stage is as important and rewarding as the assembly itself.

What truly sets Ver. Ka apart from being merely a cosmetic exercise is Katoki's deep involvement in the actual engineering and development of the kits, because unlike many designers who simply provide concept art, Katoki is himself an experienced modeler who takes CAD designs and further refines them by hand using epoxy putty, creating the master patterns from which production molds are made. His design process involves creating original drafts, using 3D printing to test proportions and articulation, and working closely with Bandai's engineers to balance aesthetics with technical feasibility. This hands-on approach ensures that Ver. Ka kits not only look exceptional but also incorporate thoughtful engineering solutions. For instance, the MG ZZ Gundam Ver. Ka required extensive work to maximize articulation while preserving the core fighter gimmick and transformation system. Katoki also pioneered the psycho frame technology for the Unicorn Gundam, which uses clear parts that reveal internal colored plastic under UV light, a gimmick that has since become iconic.

The Ver. Ka catalog reads like a greatest hits collection of the Gundam franchise, with among the most celebrated releases being the Nu Gundam Ver. Ka, widely considered one of the best Master Grade kits ever produced, and the massive Sazabi Ver. Ka, famous for its incredible detail and size. Other notable entries include the Hi-Nu Gundam Ver. Ka, the Full Armor Gundam Thunderbolt Ver. Ka with its enormous fuel tanks and weapon racks, the Unicorn Gundam Ver. Ka, the Sinanju Stein Ver. Ka, the Victory Two Gundam Ver. Ka, and the recent Wing Gundam Zero Endless Waltz Ver. Ka. Several Ver. Ka releases have even been chosen through annual fan votes, allowing the Gunpla community to directly influence which mobile suit Katoki will redesign next, creating a direct connection between the designer and the builders.

For builders, a Ver. Ka kit represents a premium experience that demands more time, care, and skill than a standard Master Grade, as the refined proportions, dense surface detail, and overwhelming decal sheets require patience and precision to complete properly. However, for those who appreciate design with intention, who want every line and marking to mean something, and who see a Gunpla kit as a canvas for something truly impressive, Ver. Ka offers a level of finishing and aesthetic cohesion that no other standard retail Gunpla release provides out of the box. It is not just a kit but a direct expression of one of the most influential mechanical designers in Gundam history!

Robot Spirits is a line of pre-built, pre-painted action figures produced by Bandai's Tamashii Nations division, and the core difference is that where Gunpla offers a creative building project, Robot Spirits offers a ready-to-play collector's item. These figures are designed for enthusiasts who want a high-quality, durable representation of a mecha straight out of the box without any of the time or skill investment required for model assembly, and as one commentator noted, if you are not a modeler who wants to build toys from scratch, Robot Spirits presents a great instant gratification option.

The line was launched in 2008 and is also known as Robot Damashii, with the name Robot Spirits intended to convey that these figures are created specifically for robot-loving collectors, embodying the passion and technology that Bandai has accumulated over the years. The figures use computer-aided design and advanced articulation engineering to achieve stunning accuracy and poseability, with the design philosophy borrowed from Bandai's successful S.H.Figuarts line of action figures. Robot Spirits is organized into several sub-lines or Sides that categorize figures by their source series, and while the primary focus is on the Real Robot genre, with the largest category being Side MS which covers mobile suits from the various Gundam meta series, the line extends far beyond Gundam to include mecha from other popular anime, with Sides dedicated to Knightmare Frames from Code Geass, Arm Slaves from Full Metal Panic, Variable Fighters from Macross, Evangelion units, and even Aura Battlers from Dunbine.

Within the Robot Spirits line, there are several notable premium sub-lines that offer elevated quality and design. The Ver. A.N.I.M.E. sub-line, introduced in 2016 starting with the RX-78-2 Gundam, focuses on anime-accurate sculpting and unprecedented articulation, and what makes these particularly special is the inclusion of extensive effect parts that allow collectors to recreate key battle scenes and famous dismemberments from the original series. For example, the GM Sniper II Ver. A.N.I.M.E. includes vernier effect parts for thrusters, curved beam saber effects, and even a functional visor that can be opened and closed. The Ka Signature sub-line represents a collaboration with renowned mechanical designer Hajime Katoki, the same designer behind the Ver. Ka Gunpla kits, and these figures feature Katoki's distinctive sharp, refined aesthetic and are available both as standard Robot Spirits releases and as Metal Robot Spirits figures, which incorporate diecast metal joints and parts for added weight and durability. Recent Ka Signature releases include the Penelope and Xi Gundam from Hathaway's Flash, as well as a prototype Rick Dias from Zeta Gundam.

In terms of scale, Robot Spirits figures are non-scale, meaning there is no consistent ratio across the line, though most Gundam figures stand approximately twelve to thirteen centimeters tall, which is roughly comparable to a 1/144 scale Gunpla kit. However, the line is not perfectly to scale, so a Knightmare Frame from Code Geass might stand at a similar height to a massive mobile suit from Gundam, which can look odd when displayed together but is a common compromise in action figure lines. Pricing for Robot Spirits figures is typically higher than a standard High Grade Gunpla kit but often lower than a Master Grade, with a standard release costing around sixty to eighty US dollars while premium sub-lines like Ka Signature or Metal Robot Spirits can easily exceed one hundred dollars, and some Tamashii web exclusive releases commanding even higher prices on the secondary market. Many figures are released as Tamashii web exclusives, meaning they are only available through Bandai's online store for a limited pre-order window, which can make them difficult to acquire after their initial release.

Gundam models with Titanium Finish totally metallic

Gundam models with a Titanium Finish are not made of metal, despite what the name might suggest, because they are still the same standard plastic injection kits as their regular counterparts. The term Titanium Finish refers instead to a special coating process that is applied to the plastic armor runners before they are packaged, which gives the outer parts a glossy, metallic sheen that looks like polished metal even though the material itself remains plastic.

What makes these kits special is that they are premium, limited edition releases designed to stand out with a luxurious look right out of the box. The main white or colored armor parts are coated to create a shiny, reflective surface similar to anodized metal, giving the kit a deluxe and premium appearance. Features like the V-fin, which is the blade antenna on the head, and the chest vents are often given a shiny semi-gloss or gold plated finish instead of the standard yellow plastic. The inner frames and weapons are typically molded in metallic colors such as gunmetal or silver rather than standard gray, which enhances the overall mechanical feel. To match this premium content, these kits usually come in beautifully designed, collector friendly boxes that differ from standard releases.

However, if you are considering purchasing a Titanium Finish kit, there are several specific challenges to keep in mind. Because the coating is applied to the runner before the parts are cut out, the sprue attachment gates, commonly known as nubs, will expose the bare plastic underneath when you remove the parts, and these marks are very difficult to hide without repainting the entire piece. Traditional model sanding will immediately destroy the beautiful finish, so you will need to use very sharp nippers and a hobby knife to clean the nubs as cleanly as possible. Applying a flat or gloss topcoat is also tricky with these kits, as it can change the reflective quality of the finish, so builders often keep them uncoated or stick to a gloss coat to preserve the shine. The price is another factor, as these exclusive kits are significantly more expensive than their standard counterparts; for example, the RG Strike Freedom Gundam Titanium Finish retails for 9,020 yen while the standard version is substantially cheaper. Most of these kits are sold as Gundam Base Limited or Premium Bandai exclusives, making them harder to find and often subject to resale market markups.

It also helps to understand how this finish compares to other similar sounding Gunpla products. Standard kits have a matte or raw plastic look, while Titanium Finish kits have a shiny, metallic, almost electroplated appearance. Metal Build figures are completely different, as they are pre-built, high-end action figures with die-cast metal frames and painted exteriors, whereas the Titanium Finish is strictly a coating on a plastic model kit that you must build yourself. The term Mechanical Finish usually refers to a dull, satin metallic finish sometimes achieved through special injection methods, while Titanium Finish is glossy and highly reflective. In short, these kits are for collectors who want an impressive out of the box shine for their display shelf and are willing to pay a premium while accepting the challenges of dealing with surface nub marks, but if you prefer to do custom painting or modifications, the standard version of the kit is a much better choice.

The manuals

You do not need to know Japanese to build a Gundam model, as the assembly instructions are almost entirely pictorial and use a system of universal symbols that are easy to understand regardless of language. The manuals are designed with a step by step visual format, so even without any English text, following the diagrams is perfectly straightforward, with each step clearly numbered and accompanied by large, simple illustrations showing exactly which pieces to attach and in what order.

While the instructions are almost entirely visual, following the pictures works seamlessly if you understand a handful of key universal symbols. You will typically encounter icons such as a circled number indicating the assembly step sequence, a big X marking parts that are not needed at that moment, a symbol showing which runner or sprue to pick a piece from, and arrows indicating the correct orientation for attaching parts. You might also see icons for parts that need to be glued, metallic sticker numbers, decal placement guides, and symbols showing that a step needs to be repeated several times for symmetrical parts. Knowing these simple icons means you can confidently build any kit, even if you cannot read a single word of the text.

Regarding the availability of English manuals, most standard Gunpla manuals do not come with extensive English translations, though you may find that more recent kits from around 2016 onwards have started to use more English phrases. The primary manuals remain in Japanese, but because the diagrams are so universally clear, the lack of translation is rarely a barrier to assembly. However, there are several excellent resources for English speaking builders who want extra guidance. If you ever lose your manual, Bandai has an official website where you can download high resolution PDF instruction manuals for many recent kits. For older or discontinued kits that are not on the official site, fans rely on community archives such as Dalong.net, which has catalogued an extensive library of manual scans for virtually every retail Gunpla kit that has been released. Another helpful resource for custom painters is Mech9.com, which offers translations of the color guides and important construction notes into English. For those who want more comprehensive English guidance, Hobby Japan has released an official English book titled NOMOKEN Extra Edition: Handbook of Gunpla Modeling, which covers everything from fundamental assembly to advanced techniques. The Gundam official website has also made available English edition guides like the Gunpla Beginner's Guide 2 and HJ Mechanics series on Amazon for builders in regions such as the United States and the United Kingdom.

Manufacturer of the Gundam models

Gundam model kits are manufactured and distributed by Bandai Spirits Company Limited, which is the toy manufacturing subsidiary of the Bandai Namco Group and is responsible for the planning, development, production, and global sales of all Gunpla products. While the brand name associated with these kits is often simply Bandai, the full corporate entity behind them is Bandai Spirits, a distinction that emerged in 2018 when Bandai Spirits was established to consolidate the company's hobby divisions, taking over the plastic model business from the broader Bandai brand to focus on high-end collector items and model kits.

The physical production of the kits is centralized at the Bandai Hobby Center located in Shizuoka City, Japan, and this facility has been the heart of Gunpla manufacturing for decades. To meet growing global demand, a new, highly advanced factory named the Bandai Hobby Center Plamo Design Industrial Institute began operations in July 2025, increasing production capacity by approximately thirty five percent, and this new facility also includes a museum where visitors can observe the production process and participate in design experiences.

In South Korea, distribution of Gundam models is done primarily through Academy. There are also some pirate copies of the genuine Bandai models in China, but the quality is very bad.

All Gundam plastic model kits, commonly known as Gunpla, are manufactured in Japan, with production centralized exclusively at the Bandai Hobby Center located in Shizuoka City, Shizuoka Prefecture, a region renowned as the heart of Japan's plastic model industry. This facility handles all planning, development, and manufacturing for the entire Gunpla product line. Bandai Spirits operates two interconnected production facilities at this Shizuoka location, the original Bandai Hobby Center which has been the primary production hub since it was completed in 2006, and a brand new facility called the Bandai Hobby Center Plamo Design Industrial Institute, or BHCPDII, which began operations in July 2025 on adjacent grounds and is designed to increase total production capacity by approximately thirty five percent compared to 2023 levels.

This commitment to domestic production is so significant that the new BHCPDII factory was built as a museum-attached factory, a concept meant to serve as a factory that fascinates. The BHCPDII Museum, which opened to the public on September 2, 2025, allows visitors to observe the actual manufacturing process, view exhibits of over four thousand Gunpla models, and even participate in model design experiences. In addition to quality control and technological innovation, centralizing production in Japan also ties into Bandai's sustainability initiatives such as the Gunpla Recycling Project, which collects and recycles used plastic runners from the manufacturing process. In summary, despite being a global phenomenon with over eight hundred million units shipped worldwide, every official Gunpla kit is still designed and manufactured in Japan, primarily at Bandai's dedicated Hobby Center complex in Shizuoka.

The correct approach to Gundam modeling

The correct approach to Gundam modeling is best captured by the philosophy often repeated within the community: Gunpla is freedom. This concept, popularized by the Gundam Build Fighters anime series, emphasizes that there is no single correct way to build and that the hobby is fundamentally about personal expression, creativity, and enjoyment. Whether your goal is to meticulously replicate a mobile suit exactly as it appears on screen or to completely transform a kit into an original creation, the correct approach is the one that brings you satisfaction.

For a beginner, the most practical path into this world of freedom is to start with a solid foundation, and the core of the Gunpla experience is the snap-fit assembly, as most modern kits are designed to be built without glue or paint, with parts molded in their correct colors. This low barrier to entry allows you to focus on the fundamentals: reading the entirely visual instruction manual, using proper tools like a pair of plastic nippers to cleanly remove parts from the runners, and cleaning up the small plastic nubs left behind with a hobby knife or sanding stick. Attempting to start with an advanced kit or skipping these basic preparation steps is a common pitfall that can lead to frustration, whereas a methodical approach, working step by step in a well lit and organized space, is highly recommended for a rewarding first build.

Once you are comfortable with the basics, the true freedom of the hobby reveals itself through a vast range of techniques that allow for limitless customization, and many builders find the process meditative and the sense of accomplishment from creating something with their own hands to be deeply addictive. The hobby naturally progresses along a spectrum of engagement from the foundational level to increasingly expressive forms. The straight build, where a kit is assembled out of the box with no modifications, is the starting point and creates a perfectly satisfying display model. From there, you can move to detailing, which involves techniques like panel lining with markers to add depth to the mechanical details, applying decals, and using a matte or gloss topcoat to give the model a professional finished look. For those who want to take their creativity further, there is customization, where you can repaint a kit in an entirely new color scheme, as in the example of transforming an HG Murasame into a Decepticon inspired custom. More advanced techniques include kitbashing, which is the art of combining parts from multiple different kits to create a unique design, scratch building new components from raw plastic, and even integrating LED units for lighting effects. The most advanced form of expression is the creation of dioramas, where painted and weathered models are placed in detailed hand built scenes to tell a story.

Choice of modeler tools and supplies

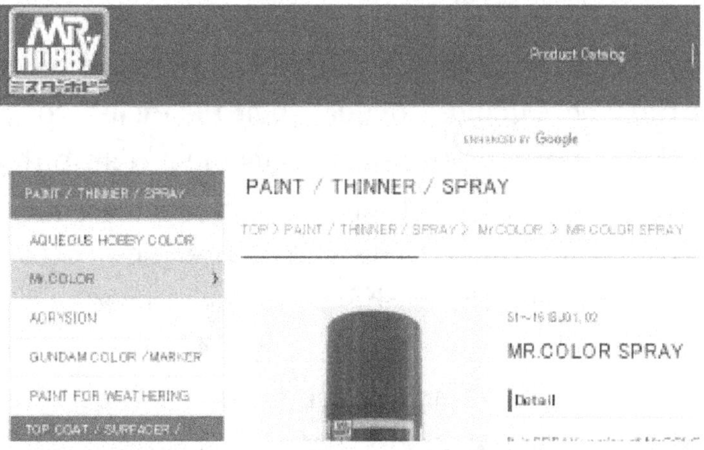

You can absolutely use tools and paints from Tamiya, Testors, and Mr. Hobby on Bandai Gundam models, and in fact these brands are widely considered the industry standard within the Gunpla community and are frequently used by builders at all skill levels. However, while the tools are universally compatible, there are a few critical precautions to take with specific types of paints and thinners to avoid damaging the plastic.

Regarding tools and cements, your basic modeling tools such as nippers, hobby knives, sanding sticks, and files will work perfectly regardless of the brand. Since Gundam kits are made of polystyrene, the same plastic used in most scale models, they also respond very well to plastic cements. You can confidently use Tamiya Extra Thin Cement or Mr. Hobby Mr. Cement on Bandai kits, as these products work by melting the plastic slightly to fuse parts together, and while Bandai kits are designed to be snap-fit, meaning assembled without glue, modelers often use these cements to eliminate seam lines on parts that are meant to be permanently joined.

When it comes to paints, primers, and thinners, you need to be aware that the plastic used in modern Bandai kits has a specific sensitivity to enamel thinners and the strong solvents found in some lacquers. Water-based acrylics, such as Tamiya Acrylics, Mr. Hobby Aqueous, and Citadel paints, are considered the safest option because they do not contain harsh solvents that attack the plastic, making them ideal for brushing, airbrushing, or hand painting details.

In fact, Mr. Hobby even produces an official Aqueous Gundam Color line specifically formulated for Gunpla. Lacquer paints, including Tamiya Lacquers and Mr. Hobby Mr. Color, provide the most durable finish but are hotter than acrylics, meaning you should apply them in thin, misted coats rather than soaking the part, as pooling thinner can cause the plastic to become brittle. Enamel paints and washes carry the highest risk because the solvents in enamel thinners and products like Tamiya Panel Line Accent Color can seep into microscopic cracks or bare plastic and cause it to crack or crumble apart, even days after application. To use enamels safely, you must first apply a gloss topcoat, preferably acrylic or lacquer, to act as a barrier between the plastic and the solvent.

Mr. Hobby also manufactures the official Gundam Marker line, which consists of felt-tip or mechanical pencil type pens designed specifically for Gunpla. These are excellent for panel lining, which adds depth to the grooves, and for touching up small details, though be aware that the paint in some pour type markers can also make plastic brittle if it pools in recesses, similar to enamel washes. In summary, you can use your Tamiya, Testors, or Mr. Hobby supplies with confidence if you use tools and cement freely without worry, use acrylic paints freely as they are ideal for base coating and detailing, always apply enamel washes like Panel Line Accent over a gloss clear coat first and never directly to bare plastic, and apply lacquer paints in light thin layers to avoid pooling.

FYI, Mr. Hobby is the primary brand name for a comprehensive line of hobby paints, tools, and accessories manufactured by the Japanese corporation GSI Creos. Originally known as Gunze Sangyo, the company rebranded to GSI Creos in 2001, and the Mr. Hobby brand has since become a global industry standard, particularly well known for its official partnership with Bandai Spirits in producing the paint colors used in Gundam model kits, with all their products being made in Japan and highly regarded by modelers worldwide.

The company's history stretches back to its founding as D. Hayashi Shoten in 1931, a silk export business that evolved through several name changes, becoming Gunze Sangyo Incorporated in 1971 and eventually GSI Creos Corporation in 2001. Over the decades, it expanded globally by opening offices in New York in 1955, West Germany in 1970, and later in China and Korea, before eventually focusing its business on the hobby market. Under the Mr. Hobby brand, the product lineup is extensive and covers nearly every aspect of the modeling process. Their paint lines are among the most famous in the hobby, including the solvent based Mr. Color line, which is praised for its durable, fast drying finish and wide color range, and the water based Aqueous Hobby Color, which is safer for hand brushing and beginner friendly. They are also the creators of the official Gundam Marker line, a series of felt tip and pour type pens designed specifically for panel lining, detailing, and touching up Gunpla models. Beyond paints and markers, Mr. Hobby produces a full range of modeling tools, including airbrushes like the Procon Boy series for spray painting, basic tool sets for beginners containing nippers and tweezers, and even practical accessories like the Mr. Apron to protect clothing during work.

Because of its deep integration with the Gundam franchise and its reputation for high quality, reliable supplies, Mr. Hobby is the go-to brand for many Gunpla builders, from beginners using a basic tool set to advanced modelers airbrushing complex custom paint schemes.

The very basic tools necessary

To start building Gundam models, you only need a few basic tools, as the kits are designed to be assembled without glue or paint right out of the box, and the essential tools for any beginner focus on cleanly removing parts from the plastic frames and handling small pieces. The single most important tool is a pair of plastic model side cutters, often called nippers, which are specifically designed to cut the small plastic connections known as gates that attach the parts to the runner. Using a proper pair of nippers helps you remove pieces cleanly and is a worthwhile investment, as standard hardware store pliers can crush or damage the delicate plastic.

After cutting a piece from the runner, there is often a small leftover bump or rough spot where the gate was attached, and to smooth this out and give the part a clean finish you will need a sanding stick, sanding sponge, or a fine file. Many builders also use a hobby or X-Acto knife to carefully trim away the last bit of the nub mark for an even cleaner result. Because Gundam kits include many small components and tiny sticker decals, a good pair of precision tweezers is essential for gripping and placing them without frustration. A self-healing cutting mat is also highly recommended, as it protects your work surface from scratches caused by knives and provides a clean, organized area to build. Finally, while not strictly a tool for the physical build, having a good desk lamp with bright lighting will make it much easier to see small details and perform precise work.

While not necessary for a simple assembly, a panel line marker is a very common beginner tool used to add depth and detail to the model's grooves and panel lines, making it look much more realistic with very little effort. Many of these basic items can be purchased individually from hobby brands like Tamiya or Mr. Hobby, but you can also find affordable all-in-one starter kits online that contain the essential nippers, knife, tweezers, and files to get you started. With this small collection of tools, you will be fully equipped to build any High Grade or Entry Grade kit successfully.

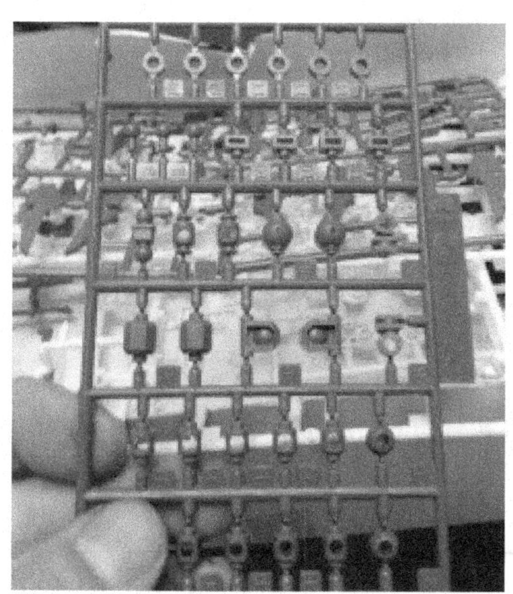

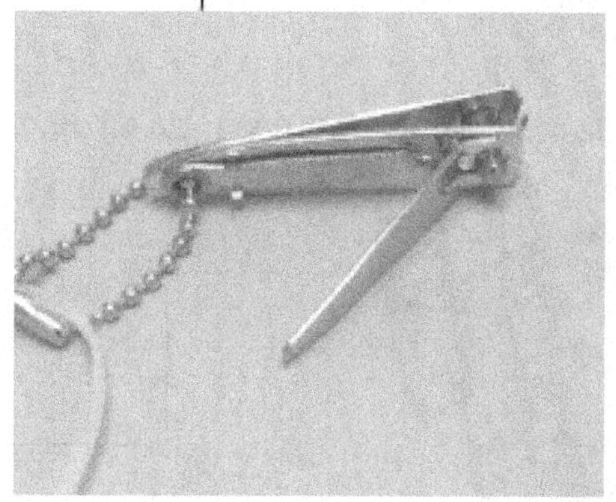

You can use a nail cutter to cut away remaining tree attachments and bumps from the model parts. A low cost substitute to side cutter.

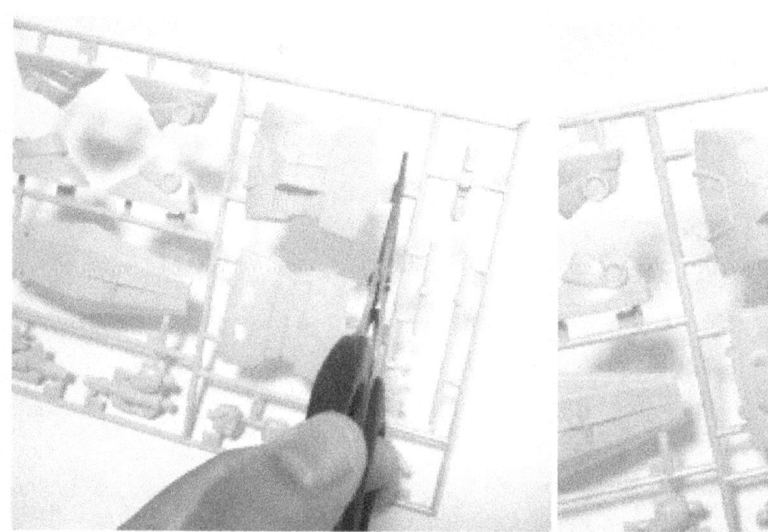

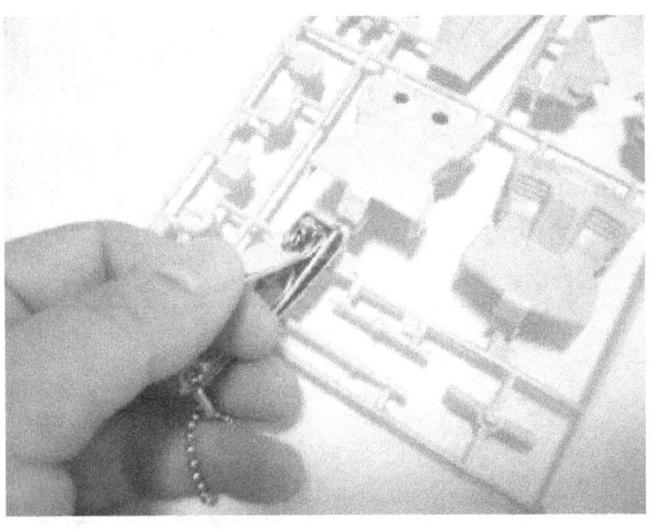

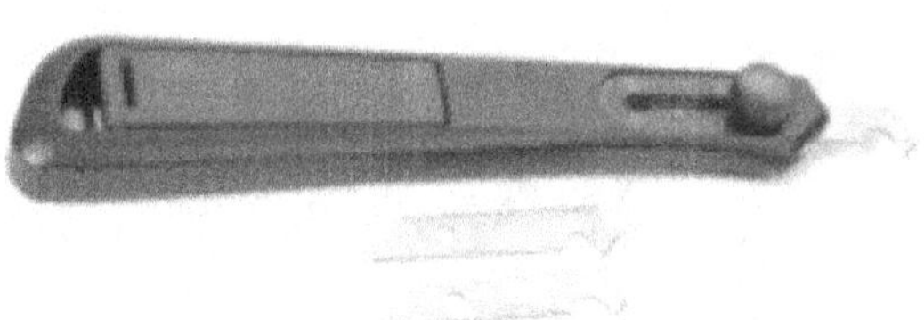

You use razor knife for task that needs a very sharp edge, such as trimming plastic. Do use it very carefully – don't cut your fingers!

For kids, knife is something to avoid. Scissors are safer for them!

When you do your cutting works you want to do so on a protective cutting mat:

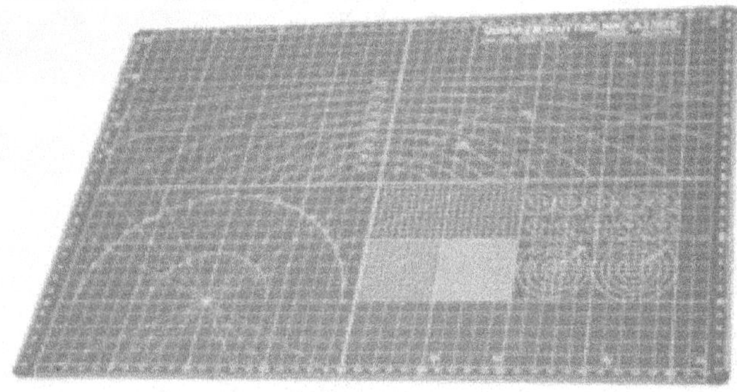

Occasionally you will come across the need to work on small screws (a few Gundam models have screws to work with). Having a set of small drivers like those shown below would definitely be beneficial.

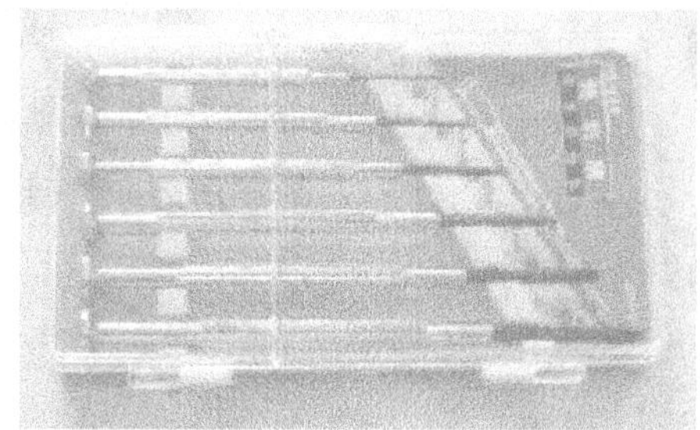

The two basic types of screwdrivers are standard (slot / flat head) screwdrivers and Philips screwdrivers. Do note that using a screwdriver of the wrong type or size may damage the screw, which may give you unexpected troubles.

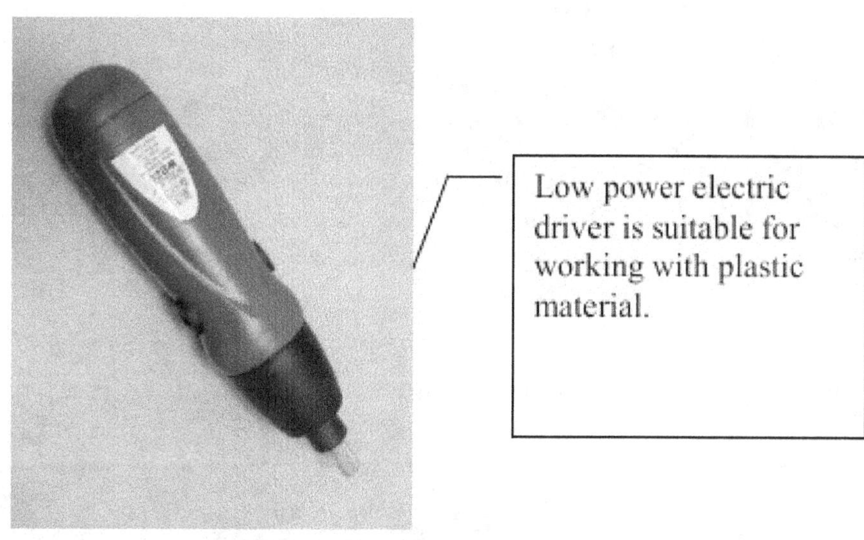

Low power electric driver is suitable for working with plastic material.

Using electric driver will definitely improve your productivity. For plastic models, a simple 3.6V electric driver will do the job. *You can in fact use the electric driver for purposes other than driving screws!*

You use sand paper (sanding sheets) for smoothing out bumps on the plastic surface. Grit size refers to the size of the particles of abrading materials that have been embedded in the sandpaper.

A number of different standards have been established for the grit sizes. The two most common are the United States CAMI and the European FEPA "P" grade. With the P grading, the larger the number the finer the sand paper you can get.

For plastic modeling you need to sand with wet sand paper. Therefore the sandpaper must be water proof.

Sanding is different from polishing so polishing cloth is of no use for sanding.

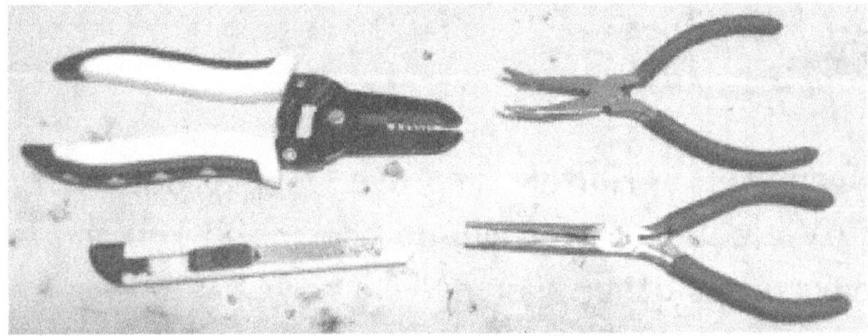

You shall need needle-nosed pliers when handling smaller parts. Combination slip-joint pliers are usually needed for handling relatively larger parts.

Progressive sanding and wet sanding

Progressive sanding and wet sanding are two advanced techniques used in model building to achieve a smooth, professional finish on plastic parts. They are often used together, especially when preparing a surface for painting or removing seam lines.

Progressive Sanding refers to the process of sanding a surface with a series of abrasives that gradually become finer. You start with a coarse, low-grit sandpaper or sanding stick, typically around 400 to 600 grit, and then move to progressively higher, finer grits, such as 800, then 1000, then 1500, and finally 2000 or higher. The purpose of this technique is to remove larger scratches, imperfections, or material quickly with the coarse grit, and then use each subsequent finer grit to erase the scratches left by the previous one. By the end of the process, you are left with a surface that has no visible scratches at all. If you were to jump straight to a fine grit, you would never remove the deep marks left by the coarse grit, but if you stop at a medium grit, you would still see sanding lines. Progressive sanding ensures that each level of scratch is completely eliminated by the next, leaving the plastic perfectly smooth and ready for painting or a glossy finish. This technique is essential for removing the nub marks left over from cutting parts off the runner, for eliminating seam lines after gluing two halves of a piece together, or for preparing clear parts like canopies and sensors to be crystal clear.

Wet Sanding is a technique that involves using water or a lubricant as a lubricant on the sandpaper or sanding sponge while you are sanding. Instead of sanding the plastic dry, you dip the sandpaper in water and keep the surface and the abrasive wet throughout the process. The water serves two important purposes: it acts as a lubricant to prevent the sandpaper from clogging with plastic dust, and it helps to carry away the fine particles so they do not scratch the surface. The primary benefit of wet sanding is that it produces a much smoother and cleaner result, especially with finer grits. Because the water flushes away the abraded plastic, you avoid the deep, random scratches that dry sanding can sometimes cause. Wet sanding is particularly crucial when working on clear parts, as dry sanding will turn them cloudy and opaque, but wet sanding can restore and even improve their transparency, allowing you to achieve a glass-like finish. It is also very effective for the final stages of progressive sanding on painted surfaces to eliminate orange peel texture before applying a final clear coat.

In practice, these two techniques are often combined. A modeler might start progressive sanding with a coarse grit, say 600, using a dry sanding stick to quickly remove a large seam line or nub mark. After that initial removal, they would likely switch to wet sanding with finer grits, such as 1000, 1500, and 2000, using a sanding sponge and water. This combination allows the coarse grit to do the heavy work quickly, while the wet sanding with fine grits provides the final, flawless, scratch-free surface that is essential for a high-quality painted or unpainted finish. Many Gunpla builders who aim for a polished, "out of the box" look on bare plastic will use progressive wet sanding up to a very high grit, such as 3000 or 4000, to achieve a subtle, satin sheen on the plastic itself.

Do remember, not all sandpaper is suitable for wet sanding! For plastic modeling, I prefer to use P1000 sand paper for fine sanding in water. This can avoid damaging the plastic surface. A coarse sandpaper can sand off too much plastic too easily. FYI, the grading is usually printed at the back of the sandpaper.

All about putty

You use model putty to fill up gaps and join lines. My personal favorite is the toothpaste-like Tamiya white putty. In the US, the most common brands of putty are Squadron Green and Testors Contour. To apply the putty, simply put

a dab on a cutter and then wipe it along the join line.

In fact, anything with a flat surface (cutter, knife...etc) can be used for applying putty. Professional modeler may prefer to use a special purpose putty applicator instead.

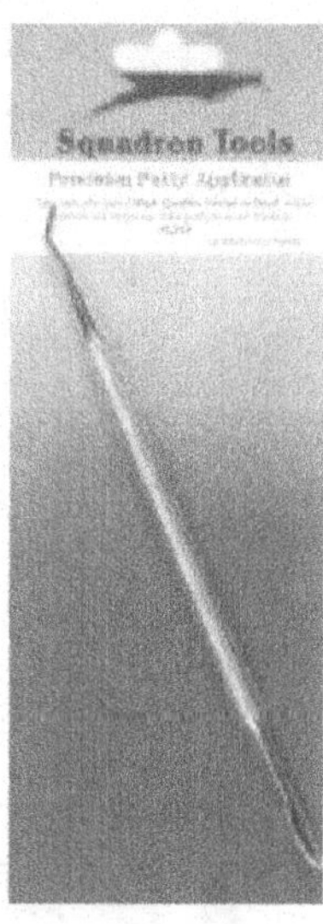

For large gaps, you may use toothpick to press the putty between the gaps. Good quality putty is highly elastic – that is, once dried it is not easy to crack. **I am very happy with the Tamiya putty so far.**

Most model putty contains toluene that can melt the plastic surface such that the putty can truly "mix" with the plastic itself. Putty that has not been dried can be removed with lacquer thinner. You may need rubber gloves when working with putty if you have sensitive skin.

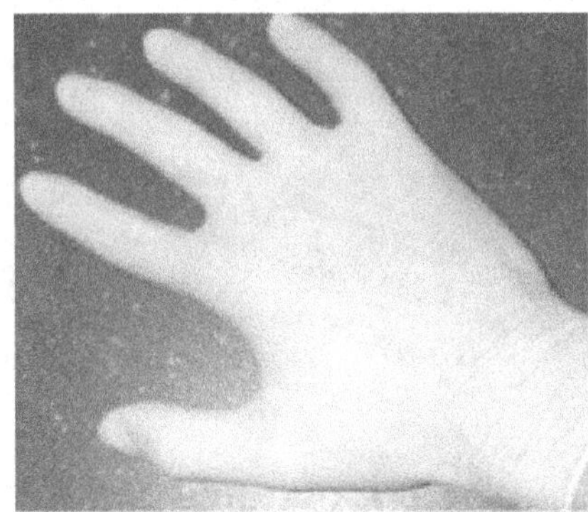

The proper way to use putty on your Gundam models begins with understanding the two main types available to modelers. The first is epoxy putty, which comes as two separate parts—a base and a hardener—that you knead together to activate. This type is strong, shrinks very little as it cures, and is ideal for filling larger gaps or even sculpting new details. The second is solvent-based putty, which comes in a single tube as a paste. It works best for filling small seam lines and hairline cracks, but because it dries by evaporation, it can shrink slightly over time.

Before you even open the putty, the most important step is to assemble the two parts using standard plastic cement, pressing them firmly together and leaving no gap. If you hold or clamp them while the cement dries, a small bead of melted plastic will often squeeze out of the seam. Sanding this bead down first may completely eliminate the gap, meaning you might not need putty at all. Only when a persistent gap remains after this treatment should you reach for the putty.

To apply solvent-based putty, squeeze a small amount onto a scrap piece of cardboard, then use a toothpick to spread a thin layer directly into the seam, slightly overfilling it to create a small ridge. It is far better to apply two thin layers than one thick one. For epoxy putty, cut equal lengths of the base and hardener and knead them together with your fingers until the color is completely uniform. Once mixed, you have a limited working time—often around thirty minutes—to press the putty into the gap before it begins to harden.

After applying the putty, patience is essential. You must let it cure completely, which typically takes at least twenty-four hours. Sanding too early will only smear the putty or ruin the surface. Once the putty is fully hardened, start sanding with a medium-grit paper such as 400 to remove the bulk of the excess. Gradually work your way up to finer grits—600, then 800, then 1000 or higher—until the surface is perfectly flush with the surrounding plastic. Run your fingernail or a toothpick across the area; if you still feel a dip or a ridge, you need to apply another thin layer of putty and repeat the sanding process.

A professional trick is to spray a thin coat of primer over the sanded area once you think it is perfect. Primer never lies—it will reveal any tiny imperfections or pinholes you might have missed, allowing you to fix them before you begin your final painting. For very fine scratches or tiny pinholes, you can also brush on a thick primer like Mr. Surfacer 500 as a final step before your main primer. Another alternative for very small or stubborn seams is to apply a tiny bead of super glue (CA glue) and sand it after it hardens. Finally, always wear a dust mask when sanding putty or primer, because the dust created is very fine and should not be inhaled. Once you master filling seams, your Gunpla will look noticeably cleaner, more professional, and much closer to a single solid piece of material.

Mr Hobby offers several different types of putty. Those with low viscosity are much easier to apply to a small area. On the other hand, liquid sealant putty (aka dissolved putty) with better viscosity is intended for smoothing out rough edges.

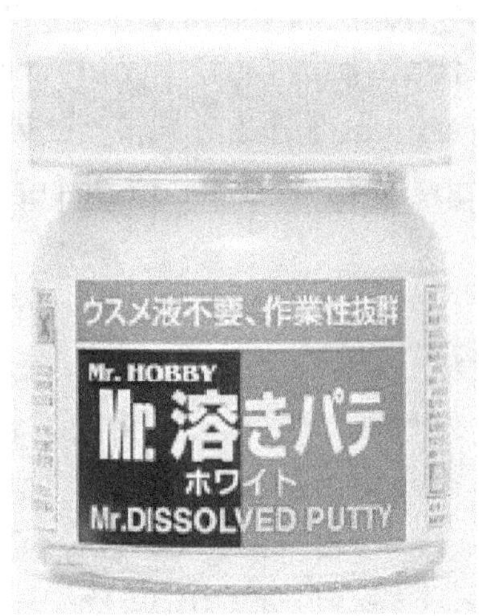

P120

MR.EPOXY PUTTY "HIGH DENSITY" TYPE

NET:78g

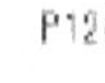 Detail

Mr.Epoxy Putty High Density Type is suitable for detailed moulding s
smooth surface on plastic parts. It is fast drying type of putty despit

Drill motor

A drill motor—usually referred to in modeling as a pin vise (manual hand drill) or a rotary tool (electric drill motor like a Dremel)—serves purposes that putty cannot achieve. Putty adds material to fill gaps, while drilling removes material to create new features or repair problems.

First, many aftermarket upgrade parts for Gundam models, such as metal thruster bells, photo-etched parts, or brass rods for added strength, require a precisely drilled hole to fit into. Without a drill, you cannot create the socket for these parts to anchor into the plastic.

Second, a drill motor is essential for fixing broken parts. If a peg that connects an arm or leg to the main body snaps off inside a joint, putty cannot fix it. The standard repair method is to drill a small hole into both broken surfaces, insert a short length of brass rod or stiff wire with super glue, and then glue the pieces back together. This technique, called pinning, creates a strong internal skeleton that makes the repair much tougher than the original plastic.

Third, drilling is used for modifying articulation and poseability. For example, if you want to add a locking mechanism to a weapon so it stays in a figure's hand, you might drill a tiny hole in the grip and a matching hole in the palm, then insert a small magnet into each. Similarly, some builders drill shallow holes in joints to insert small springs or screws that add friction, allowing a loose floppy arm to hold a heavy weapon.

Fourth, a drill motor is necessary for working with materials other than plastic. When you use epoxy putty to sculpt a new detail or fill a large gap, that putty hardens into a material much tougher than polystyrene. Sanding it is easy, but if you need to create a mechanical-looking indent or a hole in that cured putty, a standard hobby knife will struggle, but a small drill bit will cut through it cleanly.

Finally, the difference between a manual pin vise and an electric rotary tool matters. A pin vise is a small hand-held chuck that you turn with your fingers. It gives you excellent control and is perfect for drilling small, precise holes up to about two millimeters wide for pinning or metal parts. It is also very safe because you cannot accidentally tear the plastic. An electric drill motor like a Dremel, however, is used for much larger jobs, such as carving out the inside of a hollowed weapon barrel, sanding a large area with a drum sander attachment, or cutting through thick plastic. Because electric rotary tools spin very fast, they can melt or grab the plastic and ruin the part in a fraction of a second, so they are generally recommended only for experienced builders or for rough material removal before switching to hand tools for finishing.

The Tamiya handy drill kit for plastic modeling use.

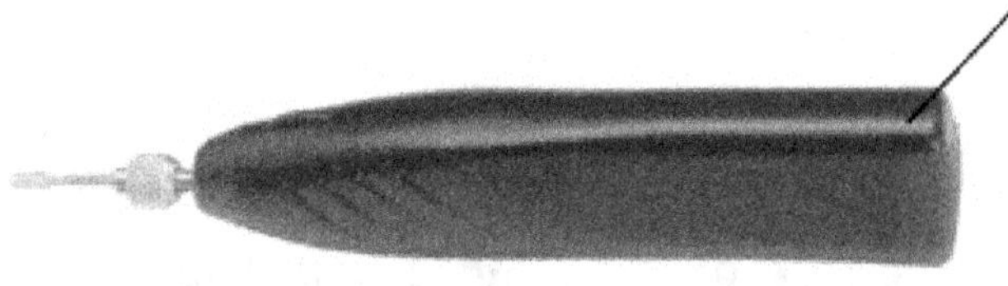

The Mr. Hobby Mr. Cordless Router can serve similar purposes.

The Tamiya basic drill set has small drill bits including 1mm, 1.5mm, 2mm, 2.5mm and 3mm.

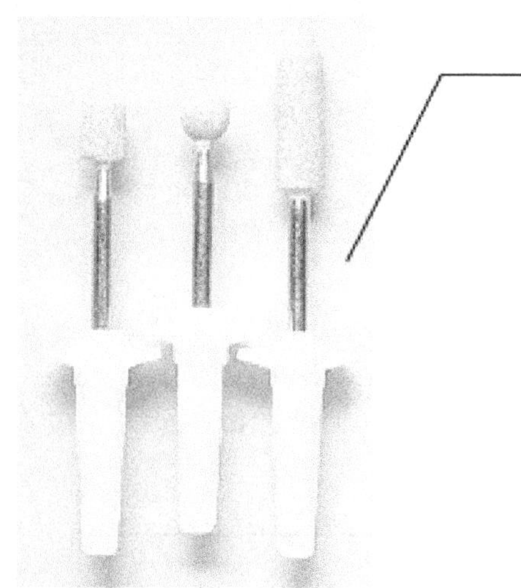

A drill press can help you drill better holes, but you should not need it unless you need to engage in high precision drill works.

Marui used to offer an electric drill set and an electric grinding set for modeling purpose. The good thing about these products is that they will never be over-powered when working on your model parts. The bad thing is that they require manual assembly prior to actual use :<

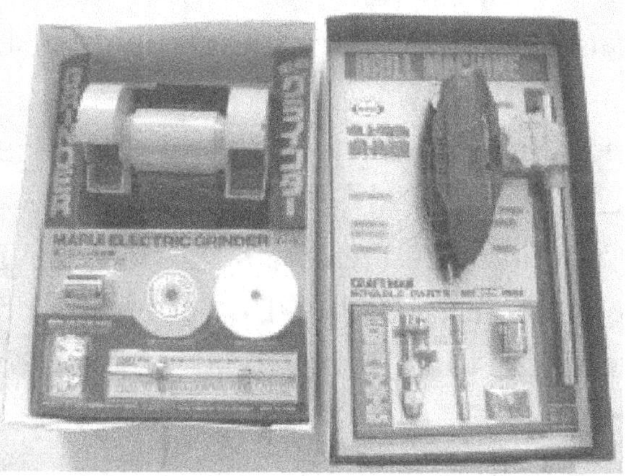

You may need some assorted files (such as straight edge, rounded and rounded side) for deburring and cleaning the edges of cuts needed for slight modification of certain parts.

Some modelers prefer to work with the help of magnifying glass. For general

Gundam modeling, it is not a must have option though.

[Great Aid for Various Work]   This head-mounted magnifying visor would free up your hands to conduct detailing work on plastic models and crafts and can also be used as a reading aid. You can wear it over glasses as well as put it on your neck when not in use. The lens itself can be raised, and size adjustment is possible by sliding the temples. The set includes 1.7x, 2x, and 2.5x lenses that have a scratch-proof coating. The large-sized lens without frame ensures a large field of vision.

The Tamiya magnifying visor

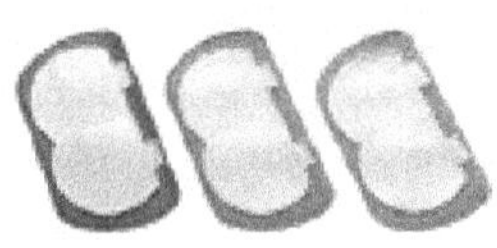

Staying organized

You need a nice place to park your tools. If you are going to work on your models regularly, consider setting up a toolbox for better organizing your tools and parts. A full blown workbench with storage stack is a good idea – it lets you keep things tidy and work in a comfortable setting.

To avoid getting into chaotic situation along your model building efforts, try to be as organized as possible. Do your work on a clean, dry and flat surface which is close enough to reach without having to walk back and forth to access the necessary tools.

Removing parts from the runner

Use a hand tool (scissors, hobby knife, cutter …etc). NEVER do it by hand. You should not attempt to cut right on the edge of the part. Try to cut away from the edge, leaving a little bit of of plastic on the part, and then begin to remove this excess plastic bit by bit.

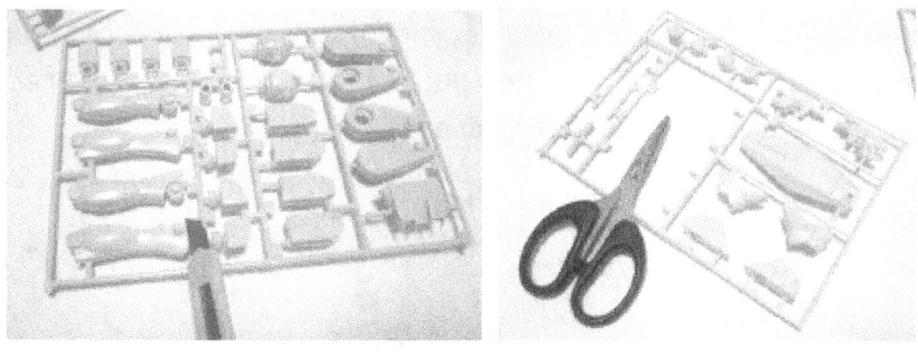

Glues

When it comes to gluing Gundam models, there is no single best glue for every job. Instead, different situations call for different types of adhesive, and knowing which one to pick is the key to a strong, clean-looking build. The three main types of glue used in Gunpla are plastic cement, super glue (also called CA glue), and epoxy glue, and each works very differently.

Plastic cement is your default choice for assembling standard polystyrene parts. It works by chemically melting and fusing the plastic pieces together at a molecular level, creating a weld that is often stronger than the surrounding plastic. For a seamless look, you can apply a small amount of thin cement, such as Tamiya Extra Thin, to the outside of a seam after the parts are pressed together; capillary action will pull the glue into the gap. The major limitation is that plastic cement only works on polystyrene, which is the main plastic in Gundam runners. It will not work on ABS plastic, metal, painted surfaces, or clear parts, and it can damage fine details if you apply too much. Strong fumes mean you should always work in a well-ventilated area.

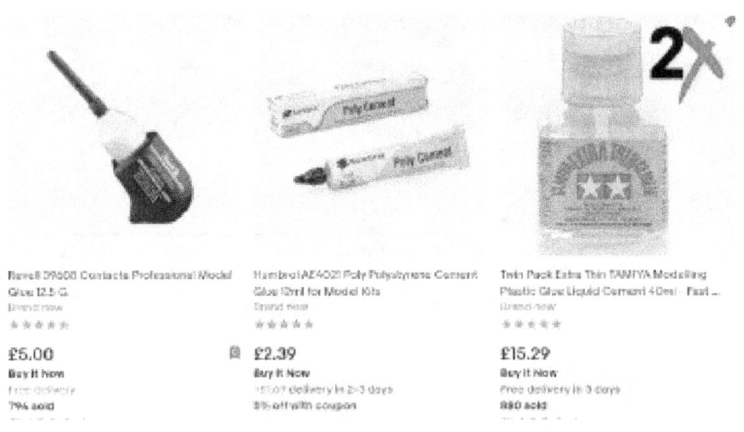

Super glue, or CA glue, is a fast-acting adhesive that creates a strong but somewhat brittle bond on the surface of the materials. Its main advantage is that it can glue different materials together, making it perfect for attaching metal parts like photo-etched details or metal thruster bells to plastic. It also works on ABS plastic and resin, and it is good for quick emergency repairs. HOWEVER, super glue can leave a white, hazy fog on clear or dark plastic surfaces if not used carefully, so thicker gel formulas are generally easier to control than thin, runny ones. For attaching metal or photo-etched parts, a tiny drop applied with a toothpick gives the best results.

Epoxy glue is a two-part adhesive consisting of a resin and a hardener that you mix together. It creates an extremely strong, durable bond and actually fills gaps well, unlike plastic cement or super glue. This makes it ideal for repairing or reinforcing high-stress joints and load-bearing parts such as hips or shoulders. It is also the best choice for pinning a broken peg, where you drill a small hole into both broken pieces, insert a short metal pin like a piece of a paperclip, and secure it with epoxy. The bond created is exceptionally tough, but epoxy takes much longer to cure—often several hours, and sometimes up to twenty-four hours for maximum strength. It also requires precise mixing of the two parts and can be messy to work with.

There are a few special cases worth mentioning. For clear parts such as beam sabers or cockpit canopies, you should never use plastic cement or super glue, as the fumes will almost certainly fog or melt the clear plastic. The safest option is a small amount of white glue, also known as PVA glue like Elmer's, which dries completely clear and can be peeled off if you make a mistake.

When fixing a broken joint, plastic cement might work for a static part, but a moving joint needs serious reinforcement. The most reliable technique is to use your drill motor to drill a small hole in both broken pieces, insert a small metal pin, and secure it with either epoxy glue or a high-strength super glue. Regardless of which glue you choose, remember that less is almost always more; a tiny amount is usually sufficient, and too much glue will result in a messy, weak bond that can ruin surface details.

Patience is a virtue—allow your glue to cure fully before handling the part. While super glue sets in seconds, plastic cement takes a few hours, and epoxy can take a full day to reach its full strength.

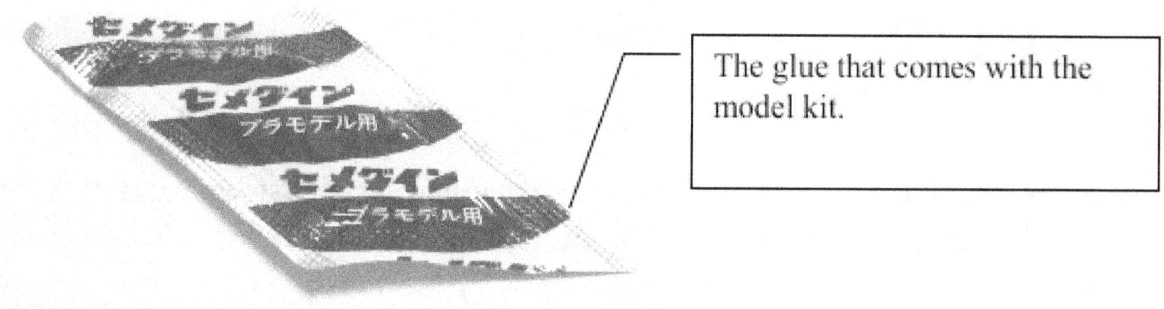

The glue that comes with the model kit.

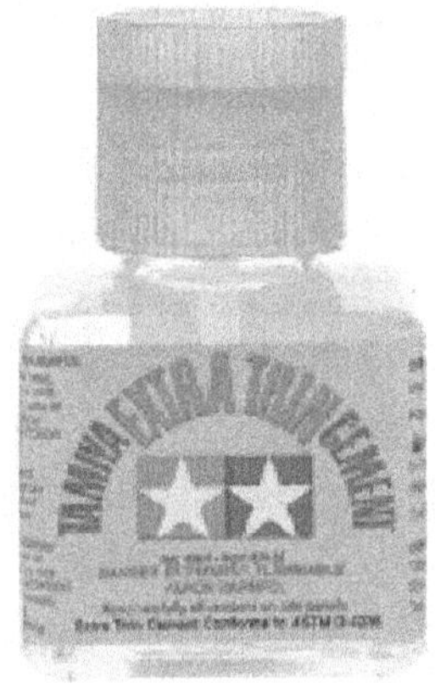

Not all glues are suitable for plastic model building. Professional model shops sell plastic liquid glues specially designed for plastic modeling. These glues usually have a brush built-in the lid. They work by melting the plastics and then fusing them together. They do not dry as fast as the typical furniture fixing glue. However, they are very easy and flexible to apply.

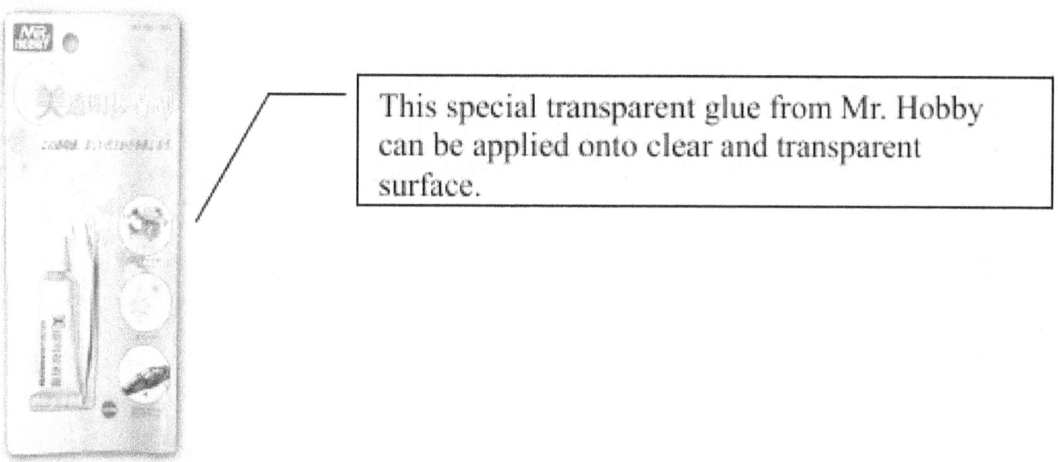

You should not always need to use the rapid-dry kind of super glue. Even though the super glue dries very fast (practically within a minute), any mistake made along the gluing process will be quite difficult to undo.

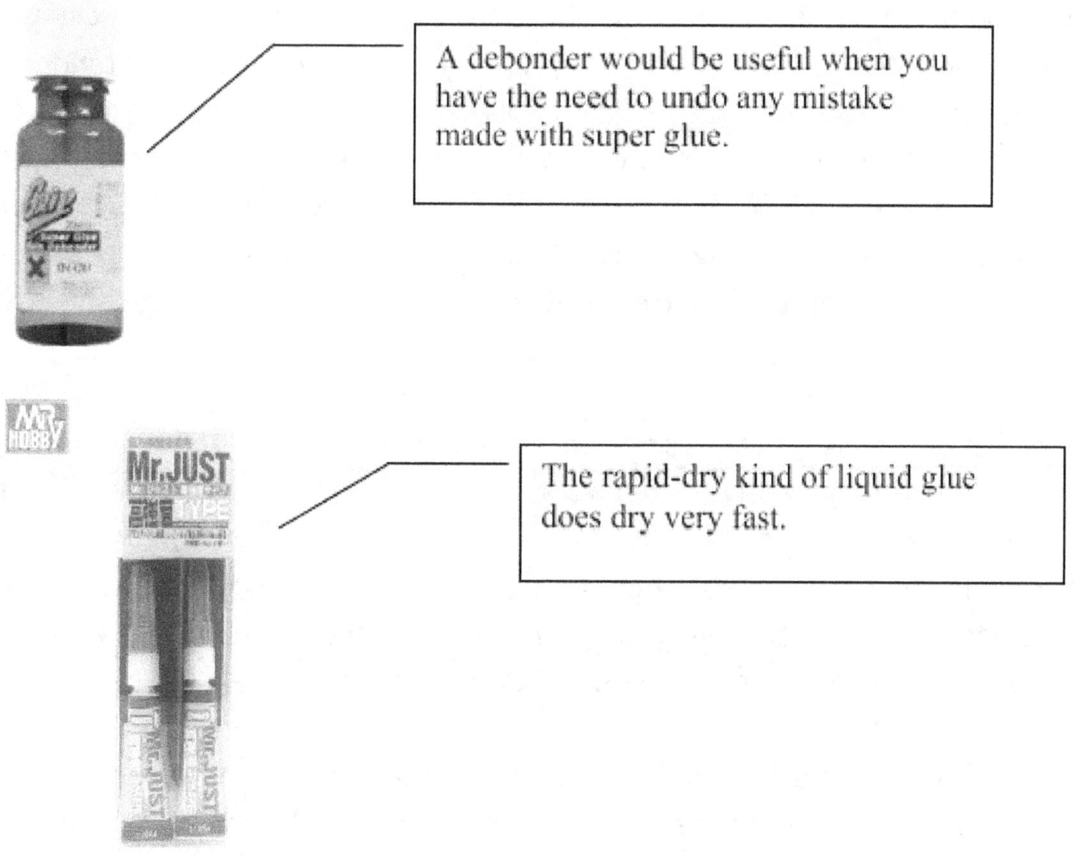

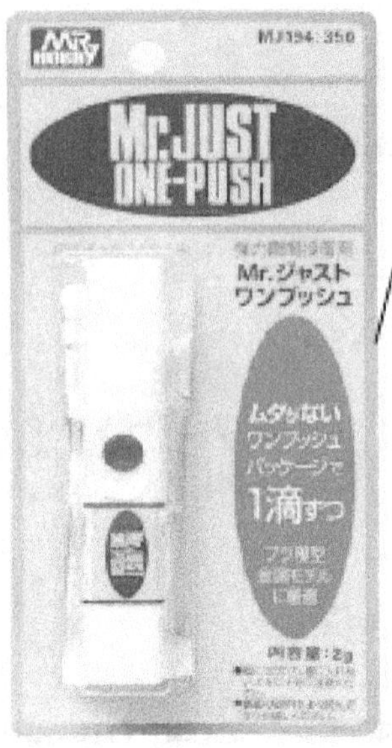

The Mr. Just liquid glue also dries very fast. It also offers very strong holding power.

Poly cement is simply another name for plastic cement, the standard glue used for assembling plastic model kits like Gundam. The "poly" is short for polystyrene, which is the type of plastic that most model kits, including Gunpla runners, are made from. Poly cement works very differently from standard super glue because it does not just stick to the surface of parts. Instead, it chemically melts the plastic. You apply the cement to the parts, press them together, and the melted surfaces fuse at a molecular level. When the cement dries, the two pieces have become a single, solid piece of plastic. This process is called solvent welding, and it creates a bond that is often stronger than the surrounding plastic itself.

Because it melts and fuses the plastic, poly cement is perfect for eliminating seam lines. When used correctly, it allows you to create a seamless joint that looks like it was never assembled in the first place. For Gundam modelers aiming for a clean, realistic finish, this is an essential tool. Another advantage is that poly cement is quite forgiving, as it gives you a short amount of time to adjust the position of parts before the bond begins to set.

However, poly cement has a few major limitations that you need to remember. First, it will instantly frost or melt clear plastic parts like beam sabers or cockpit canopies, so you must never use it on them. Second, it does not work well on painted or chrome-plated surfaces because the cement cannot penetrate the coating to reach the bare plastic underneath. Finally, you should always use poly cement in a well-ventilated area, as the fumes are strong and the liquid itself is highly flammable.

Poly cement comes in a few different forms for different tasks. Tube cements are thick and give you more time to position parts, making them a good choice for beginners or for assembling large pieces. Precision bottles with thin metal needles, such as Revell Contacta, allow for very accurate application on small, detailed parts. Extra-thin liquid cements like Tamiya Extra Thin are applied by holding the parts together and touching a brush to the seam, where the glue is then pulled into the joint by capillary action. This extra-thin type is the preferred choice for eliminating seam lines on Gunpla because it creates an extremely clean bond with very little mess.

Epoxy is intended for application which requires very strong bonding power. For general Gundam modeling you seldom need to use Epoxy. Epoxy glue may be ideal if you need to create custom joints for your model. Custom joints usually have no solid body support so strong bonding power would be necessary.

This special Mr. Just glue is for use primarily with metallic parts (although it can be applied onto plastic surface without any problem).

Keep in mind, you need proper ventilation in your work place when using plastic glue. The glue smells bad and can be harmful.

While it is understandable to want to use what you already have at home, you should avoid using hardware store cement or hot glue on your Gundam models. The cement sold at local hardware stores is almost always formulated for PVC pipes or ABS plumbing fittings, not for the polystyrene plastic used in Gundam models. Although the name "plastic cement" might sound the same, the chemical composition is completely different. Hardware store cements are extremely strong solvents designed to melt heavy-duty plumbing plastic, and when applied to the thin, delicate polystyrene of a Gundam runner, they will not simply fuse the parts; they will often dissolve them entirely, turning fine details into a mushy, gooey mess. These cements can be so aggressive that they cause the plastic to warp, bubble, or crack, permanently destroying any panel lines, vents, or mechanical details on the surface. Furthermore, they do not evaporate cleanly and often leave a thick, messy residue that is impossible to sand or paint over. In short, using hardware store cement on a Gunpla is very likely to ruin the part beyond repair, so you should only use cement specifically labeled for polystyrene model kits, such as Tamiya, Mr. Hobby, or Revell.

Hot glue is equally unsuitable, though for different reasons. Hot glue is a thermoplastic adhesive that is applied in a molten state using a glue gun and works by cooling and hardening physically, rather than by chemically bonding to the surface. Because it creates a very thick, bulky layer of adhesive, it is far too thick for Gunpla parts, which are designed to fit together with tight, precise tolerances. A layer of hot glue will force the parts apart, creating large, unsightly gaps and preventing a proper fit. For the glue to hold any strength, you need a large surface area, so on a small peg or a thin connector, the glue cannot get enough purchase, and the bond will be incredibly weak, likely breaking immediately when you try to pose the model. Hot glue also dries into hard, rubbery strands that are very difficult to remove from the nooks and crannies of a model. You cannot sand it smooth, and paint does not adhere to it well. One of the primary uses of glue in Gunpla is to fuse parts together to eliminate the seam line, but because hot glue does not melt or fuse the plastic, it is impossible to sand the joint flush, and you will always be left with a visible, glue-filled crack. The one exception where hot glue is actually useful is for non-assembly tasks: you can use it to create a temporary, protective mask for clear parts or detailed areas before spray painting. You simply apply the hot glue, let it cool, paint the model, and then peel the solid glue blob off. For actual gluing, however, it is entirely unsuitable.

For any Gundam model, you should use either poly cement for permanently fusing polystyrene parts and eliminating seams, or super glue for attaching different materials like metal to plastic or for quick repairs.

The proper way to apply plastic glue

Preparation is key. Before you apply any glue, you should always test fit the two parts together without glue. This allows you to see how they align and identify any tight spots or imperfections. You should also clean the contact surfaces of any dust, oils from your fingers, or mold release agent, as these can weaken the bond. A simple wipe with a cloth or a quick rinse with mild soap and water is usually sufficient. When you are ready to glue, the most important rule to remember is that less is almost always more. Plastic glue works by melting the plastic, so a tiny, thin layer is all that is needed to create a molecular weld. Applying too much glue will not make the bond stronger; instead, it will cause the plastic to become overly soft and mushy, leading to warped parts, melted surface details, and excess glue squeezing out of the seam. A single small drop is often enough for most Gunpla joints and connections.

The application method depends on the type of plastic glue you are using. For thick tube cements, you should squeeze a small amount onto a scrap piece of cardboard or an old plastic lid. Then, use a toothpick or the tip of a metal needle to pick up a tiny amount and spread it thinly onto one of the mating surfaces. Press the two parts together firmly and hold them for about fifteen to thirty seconds until the glue begins to set. You can then set the assembly aside to cure fully.

For precision bottle glues that come with a thin metal needle applicator, such as Revell Contacta, you can apply the glue directly from the bottle. Gently squeeze a very thin, continuous line along one of the contact surfaces, then press the parts together. The needle allows for excellent control, but you still need to be cautious not to release too much glue at once. If the needle becomes clogged, you can clear it by holding a lighter flame to the tip for a moment to burn away the dried glue.

For extra-thin liquid cements like Tamiya Extra Thin, the technique is different and is widely preferred for eliminating seam lines. You first press the two parts together without any glue, holding them firmly so the seam is closed. Then, you touch the brush applicator to the very edge of the seam. The glue is so thin that it is pulled into the gap by capillary action, flowing along the entire joint on its own. You only need to touch the brush to one or two points along a seam, and the glue will spread itself throughout. This method produces incredibly clean bonds with no excess glue on the surface. However, you must be careful not to let the glue flow into any moving joints, hinges, or areas that are meant to rotate, as it will fuse them solid. After you press the parts together, you will often see a small bead of molten plastic squeeze out of the seam. This is actually a good sign, as it means the plastic has melted and fused properly. Do not touch this bead or try to wipe it away while it is wet, as this will only smear the softened plastic across the surface. Instead, allow the glue to cure completely, which typically takes at least a few hours and ideally twenty-four hours for maximum strength. Once the glue is fully hardened, you can sand that bead of melted plastic away gently with fine-grit sandpaper, resulting in a perfectly seamless joint.

For moving parts such as knees, elbows, or shoulder joints, you need to be extremely careful. You should apply glue only to the contact surfaces that are meant to be permanently fixed, while keeping the glue far away from any hinge pins, polycaps, or areas that need to rotate. If you accidentally glue a moving joint, you can sometimes free it by applying a tiny amount of extra-thin cement to the joint and working it back and forth repeatedly, but this is risky and often damages the part. Prevention is always better than cure.

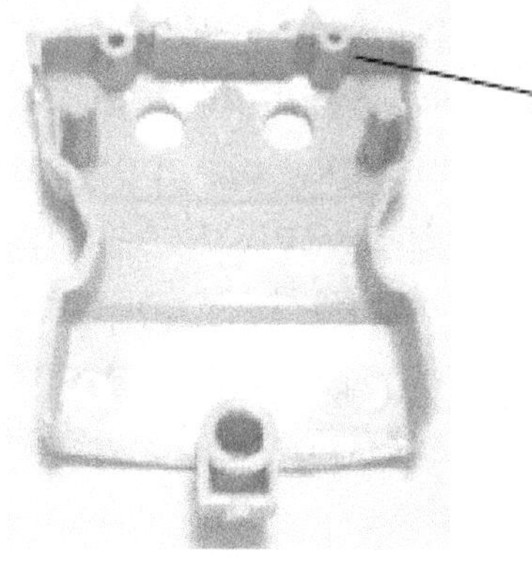

For parts that can be snapped together, you do not have to glue them but you absolutely can (and for certain results, you should). To understand the decision, you first need to know why Bandai designs Gundam kits to snap together without glue. The primary reason is accessibility. Snap-fit assembly allows beginners and younger builders to enjoy the hobby without needing any tools or chemicals. It also means you can disassemble a kit later for painting or modifications. Finally, snap-fit parts are designed with slight tolerances to create friction, which gives the model its articulation and allows you to pose it without the joints falling apart. However, even the best snap-fit design has limitations. The main problem is that snapped-together parts rarely form a completely invisible seam. If you look closely at a snap-built Gundam, you will usually see a very fine line running along the side of the leg, the arm, or the weapon. This is where the two halves of the mold meet. For a builder who wants a realistic, seamless appearance, that line is an imperfection that needs to be eliminated. Gluing the parts together with plastic cement is the only way to fuse them into a single piece so that, after sanding, the seam disappears entirely.

There are also structural reasons to glue snap-fit parts. Some parts, particularly on larger or older kits, may be prone to falling off during posing. Gluing them permanently solves this problem. Similarly, parts that hold heavy weapons or support a lot of weight, such as shoulder joints or hip connections, can benefit from the added strength of a chemical weld. A glued joint is simply much stronger than a snapped-together one.

That said, there are valid reasons to avoid gluing snap-fit parts. If you are a beginner building your first few kits, you might prefer to keep them unglued so you can take them apart later to practice panel lining, painting, or applying decals. Some builders also enjoy the ability to swap parts between different Gundam models to create custom combinations, and gluing parts together permanently prevents this. Finally, for high-articulation poses, you may want the ability to disassemble a section to adjust an inner frame component, which gluing would prevent.

The best approach is to be selective. Most experienced Gundam modelers do not glue every single snap-fit part on a kit. Instead, they glue specific areas where a seamless finish matters most. For example, you would typically glue the two halves of the thigh, the forearm, the upper arm, the torso, the front and back skirts, and any large weapon parts. These areas have visible seams that run right across visible surfaces. However, you would not glue parts that enclose an inner frame, such as the sides of the calf, because those parts need to remain separate to allow the knee joint to move freely. You would also avoid gluing any parts that are meant to rotate or slide, such as the joint covers on the elbows or the sliding mechanisms on transformation gimmicks.

Distinguishing between the earlier releases and the newer releases

Distinguishing between earlier and newer releases of Gundam models is an excellent skill to develop, as it helps you understand what to expect from a kit in terms of engineering, articulation, and overall build quality. Fortunately, Bandai provides several clear indicators that make this distinction straightforward once you know what to look for.

The most reliable method is to look for the copyright date printed on the box and the instruction manual. This is typically the year the specific kit was engineered and released, not just the year the anime series aired. For example, a kit showing a copyright of 1995 is an early Master Grade release with the engineering standards of that era, while a kit with a 2010 copyright is a much newer design. You can find this date on the front or side of the box, usually near the Bandai logo, and prominently on the first page of the instruction booklet.

Beyond the copyright date, the grade and sub-line of the kit tell you a great deal about its age and sophistication. The major grade families were introduced in a specific order, so knowing when a grade launched gives you a benchmark. The first No Grade kits appeared in 1980. High Grade arrived in 1990, Master Grade in 1995, Perfect Grade in 1998, High Grade Universal Century in 1999, Real Grade in 2010, and RE/100 in 2014. If you are looking at a Master Grade kit, a 2.0 or 3.0 designation on the box is a very clear sign of a newer, completely re-engineered version of an older kit, featuring vastly improved articulation and internal detail compared to its version 1.0 predecessor. Similarly, a Ver. Ka designation indicates a kit personally overseen by the designer Hajime Katoki, known for dense decal sheets and distinctive proportion adjustments; these started appearing in 2002 and many are considered modern classics, though the label itself does not guarantee a recent release date.

Another major distinction between older and newer kits is their approach to assembly. Kits from the 1980s and early 1990s were often designed with the expectation that the builder would use glue and paint to achieve the final look. In contrast, the modern philosophy of Gunpla, which solidified in the late 1990s and is standard today, is no glue and no paint. Newer kits are designed to snap together firmly and feature excellent color separation, meaning the parts are molded in the correct colors so they look accurate straight off the runner. When researching a kit online, product descriptions for modern kits will almost always highlight snap-fit assembly and pre-colored parts, whereas descriptions for older kits may explicitly state that paint and cement are required. The level of articulation is another key indicator, with newer kits featuring advanced joint systems for dynamic posing, while older kits are often much more static. The box design itself can be a clue, though it is less definitive than the other indicators. Bandai periodically updates box art across all grades, so while a very old kit from the 1980s will have a distinctively vintage look, a kit from 2005 might have received new box art that makes it appear more modern than it actually is. For this reason, the copyright date and the specific version number remain your most trusted tools.

All about runner frame

All Gundam model kits come with runner frames. In an injection mold, a runner is a feed channel for connecting the sprue with the cavity gate for purpose of molding. The plastic piece formed in this channel is also known as the runner frame. To be precise, the tree-like runner frame is produced along the modeling process; hot plastic is being injected into the mold through small conduits known as gates. At the end of the gates the plastic enters the mold for forming the final part of the model kit.

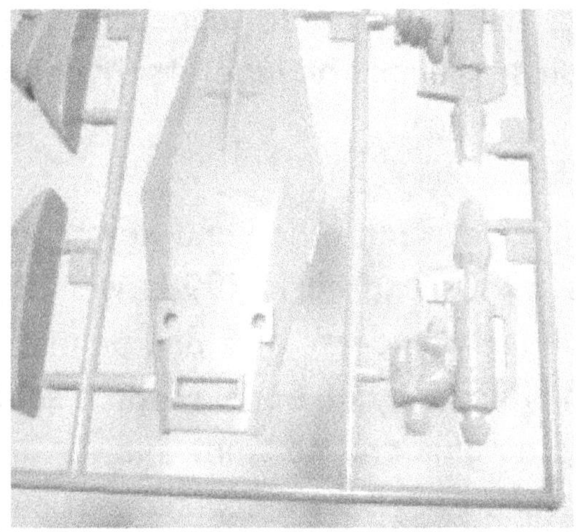

Runnerless molding is possible, but it is never implemented in the world of Gundam plastic modeling.

Steps shown in the manual

The Gundam model kit manual always begins with a visual key or legend. This section shows you the symbols that will appear throughout the instructions, such as a pair of nippers indicating where to cut the part from the runner, a small bottle indicating where to apply glue (though this is rare on modern kits), a sanding block indicating where you may need to clean a nub mark, and arrows showing which direction to slide or rotate a part. It is worth spending a minute studying this legend before you begin, as it explains the small icons you will see on every page.

After the legend, the manual typically shows a diagram of all the runners included in the box. Each runner is labeled with a letter, such as A, B, C, and so on, and the diagram clearly shows the shape of each runner and the color of the plastic. This section is extremely useful for two reasons. First, you can check that your box contains all the correct runners before you start building, which is important for confirming you did not receive a defective kit. Second, when a later assembly step tells you to find part number A12, you can look back at this runner map to confirm which runner is labeled A and roughly where on that runner part A12 is located.

The core of the manual is the assembly sequence, which is shown as a series of step-by-step illustrations. Each step is presented in a numbered box or a small panel. The first few steps will show you how to assemble the torso or the head, and the manual then builds outward to the arms, legs, and finally the weapons and accessories. Within each step, the manual uses a very specific visual language. New parts being added in that step are usually drawn in full detail, while parts that have already been assembled in previous steps are shown as simple outlines or ghosts. This makes it very easy to see exactly what you need to add and where it goes.

Every time a part is needed, the manual shows a small image of the runner letter and the part number next to the part itself. For example, you will see a small box containing the letter B and the number 7, indicating that you need part B7. The manual also uses arrows to show exactly how the part should be oriented and which direction to push or snap it into place. If an arrow curves, it means you need to rotate the part. If an arrow is straight, it means you need to slide or press the part directly into position. Some steps will also show a magnified close-up view of a particularly tricky connection, such as a small peg fitting into a tight hole, to give you a better look at the alignment.

As you work through the manual, you will also encounter symbols warning you about common mistakes. A red circle with a line through it over a pair of nippers indicates that you should not cut the part off the runner at that specific point, often because you need to cut it in two separate steps to avoid damaging a delicate piece. A warning triangle with an exclamation mark alerts you to a step that requires extra care, such as inserting a part in only one specific orientation. For polycaps, which are the soft rubbery joint pieces, the manual will often show a symbol indicating that you should press them in firmly but without forcing them, as they can be easily torn if mishandled.

The final pages of the manual are reserved for the finishing steps. These include diagrams showing you how to apply the sticker sheet or water-slide decals, indicating exactly where each marking should be placed on the model. The manual will then show you a complete exploded view of the finished model, with all the parts assembled, so you can see how everything fits together. Finally, there is often a small section showing you a few signature poses for the kit, which serves both as inspiration and as a confirmation that you have assembled all the joints correctly, because the model should be able to replicate the poses shown.

You should follow the manual in strict page order and never skip ahead. Build the head completely, then the torso, then the waist, then the arms, then the legs, and finally the accessories. Many builders make the mistake of assembling both arms at once or jumping ahead to the legs, but the manual is designed so that later steps often require parts from earlier assemblies, and working out of order can cause confusion. Take your time, study each diagram carefully before cutting any parts, and you will find that the manual guides you through every step of the build with clarity and precision.

Always make sure you understand the directions thoroughly prior to assembling the parts.

Advanced modelers do not need to follow the steps since they may come up with their very own joints connection plan.

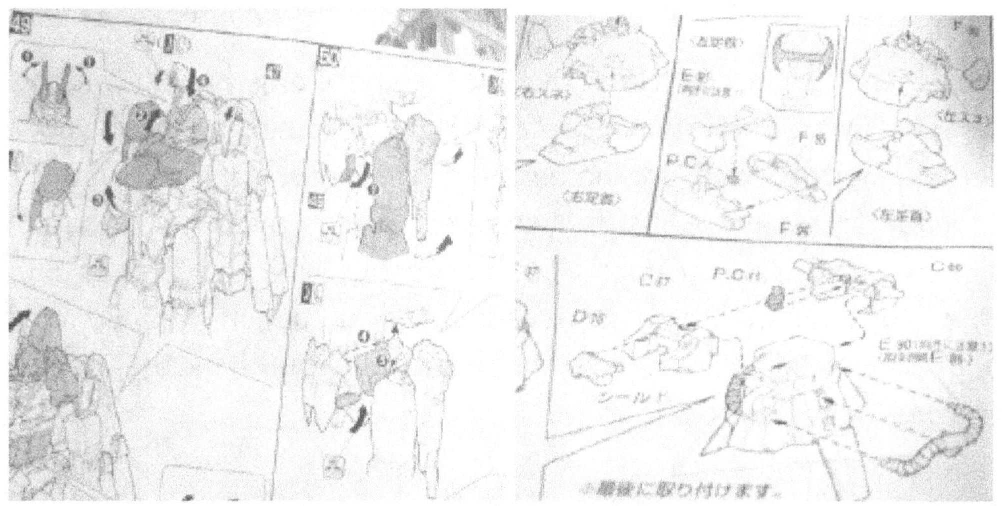

You should almost never remove all the parts from the runners before you start assembling. While it might seem efficient to get all the pieces laid out and ready, this practice actually creates many more problems than it solves for a Gundam modeler.

The primary reason to leave parts on the runners is organization and identification. A Gundam kit can have anywhere from a few dozen to over a hundred individual parts, and many of them look very similar to one another. The runners are lettered, and each part has a number next to it. The instruction manual tells you exactly which runner letter and part number you need for each step, for example, "A1" or "B23." If you cut all the parts off first, you will be left with a pile of identical-looking grey, white, or blue plastic pieces with no way to tell which is which. You would then have to waste a great deal of time holding each piece up to the manual's diagrams to try to match its shape, which is frustrating and prone to mistakes.

The second major reason is that the runners keep small parts safe. A tiny piece like a cheek vent, a small thruster nozzle, or a delicate v-fin is easy to lose on a workbench or floor when it is loose. While attached to the runner, it is securely held in place and much harder to misplace or accidentally knock onto the floor. Cutting parts off one step at a time means you only have a few loose pieces to manage at any given moment.

Third, leaving parts on the runners helps you follow the assembly sequence correctly. The instruction manual is carefully designed so that you assemble the model in a logical order, adding parts in layers. For example, you might need to fit an inner frame piece inside two outer armor pieces. If you cut all the armor pieces off first, you might not remember which one goes on the left versus the right, or which layer is supposed to go on top. By cutting and assembling each step as it comes, you naturally build in the correct order without having to re-sort a pile of parts.

There is one very specific exception where removing all parts from the runners first is actually necessary, and that is when you plan to fully paint the entire model. Many advanced painters will cut every single part off the runners, clean up the nubs, and then attach each part to a small alligator clip on a stick for painting. They do this because the part of a piece that connects to the runner cannot be painted while it is still attached, and painting on the runner leaves an unpainted spot after assembly. However, this is an advanced technique for experienced builders who have already memorized what every part looks like and where it goes. For a standard snap-build or a first few kits, you should never do this.

The correct workflow is to keep the runners organized on your desk or in a runner stand. You then follow the instruction manual step by step. For each step, you locate the required runner, find the part number called out in the diagram, cut that specific piece off using your nippers, clean up the nub mark with a hobby knife or sandpaper, and then assemble it immediately. Then you move on to the next step. This method keeps your workspace tidy, prevents lost parts, ensures you build in the correct order, and makes the entire process much more enjoyable and less stressful.

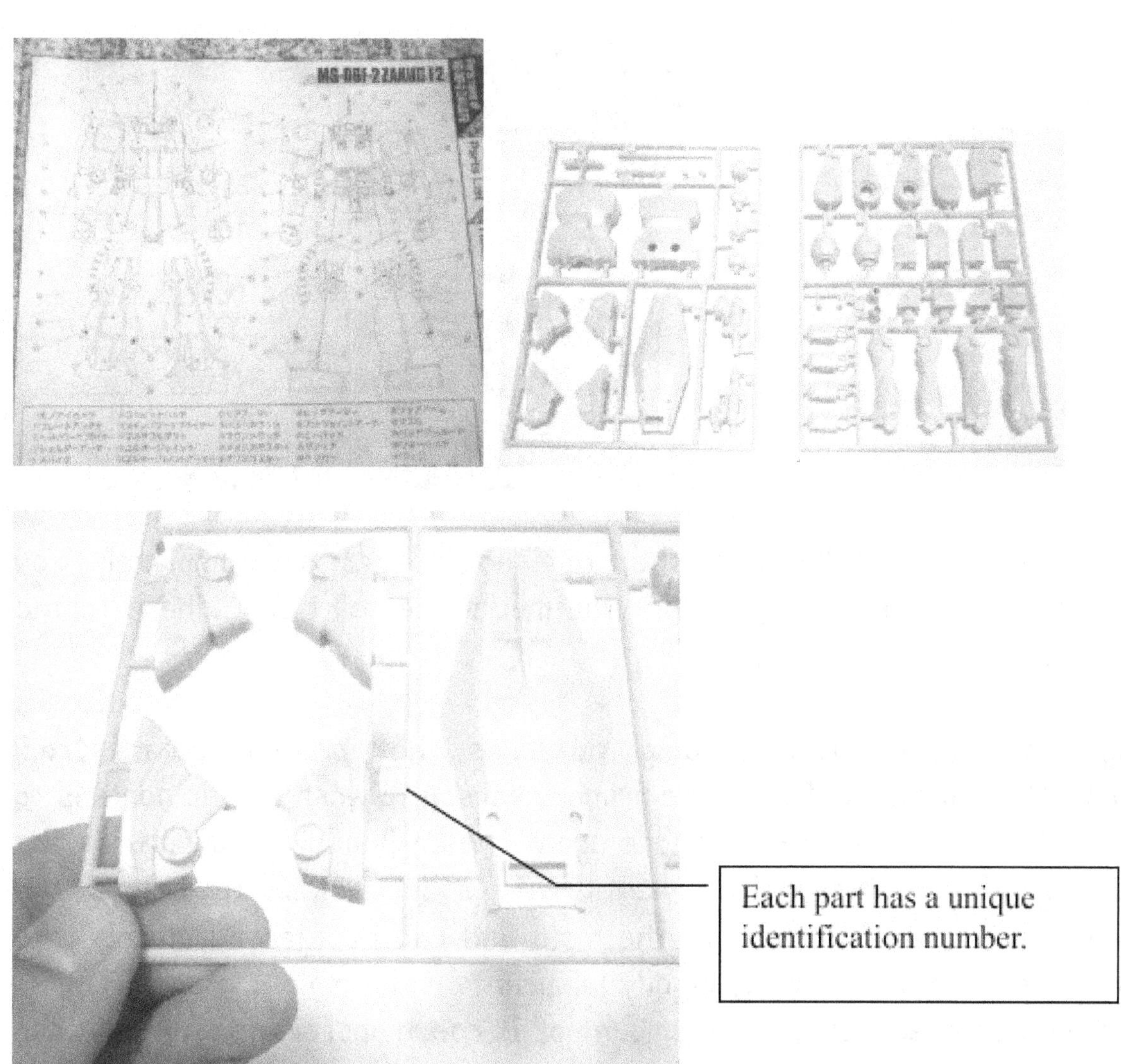

Parts cleansing

After inspecting the kit, you may wash the plastic parts in warm soapy water.
Use warm water. Liquid cleaner for general housekeeping purpose would do just
fine.

Do this gently and carefully. Rinse them off and let them dry completely. You do this now so later on when you paint the model the paint can adhere to the plastic easier.

Washing can remove those bonding materials that prevent paints from sticking to the plastic surface. The primary reason to wash plastic parts is to remove a substance called mold release agent. When Bandai manufactures the runners, they inject hot molten plastic into steel molds. To ensure the solidified plastic does not stick to the mold and can be ejected cleanly, the factory applies a very thin, waxy or oily lubricant to the mold surfaces. This is the mold release agent, and a tiny amount of it can transfer onto the surface of every part on every runner.

For most builders, this residual mold release agent is not a problem. You can snap the kit together, apply panel liners, and even topcoat the model without noticing any issues. However, the mold release agent becomes a serious problem if you plan to paint your Gundam. Paint adheres to surfaces through mechanical and chemical bonding, and a layer of waxy oil prevents that bond from forming. If you paint directly over unwashed parts, the paint may bead up, fail to cover evenly, or peel off easily after it dries. Washing removes this invisible barrier and gives you a clean, paint-ready surface.

There is a secondary reason to wash parts, which is to remove dust and fingerprints that accumulate during handling. As you cut, sand, and test-fit parts, you will inevitably leave small amounts of oil from your fingers and fine plastic dust from sanding on the surfaces. A quick wash removes these contaminants as well, ensuring a perfectly clean surface for painting or even for applying decals.

You should absolutely wash the parts if you plan to do any painting, whether you are using spray cans, an airbrush, or hand brushing. The few minutes of washing will save you from the frustration of paint that refuses to stick or that chips off later. You should also consider washing if you are building a very old kit from the 1980s or early 1990s, as older manufacturing processes sometimes left heavier residues of mold release.

For a modern Bandai kit that you are building straight out of the box with no painting, washing is generally unnecessary and adds little benefit, as the tiny amount of mold release is unlikely to affect panel liners or decals.

There are valid reasons to skip washing. First, water and small, delicate parts can be a bad combination. Very small pieces, such as the fine vents on a Real Grade or the tiny sensors on a Perfect Grade, can easily fall off a drying rack or get lost down a drain. Second, washing adds time and effort to your build, and if you are simply snap-building for relaxation, the benefit is minimal. Third, some builders argue that handling the parts after washing puts new oils back onto the plastic anyway, so the benefit is temporary unless you wear gloves during assembly.

If, however, you have no plan to paint the model, you may skip this washing process entirely.

Plan your painitng scheme

While it is a good idea to figure out the painting scheme early, we seldom paint the parts while they are still on the runner frame.

When you paint a part while it is still attached to the runner, you create a beautiful, uninterrupted coat of paint over the entire visible surface of that part. The problem arises the moment you need to remove the part from the runner. Every plastic part is connected to the runner frame by one or more small gates, which are the points where the molten plastic flowed into the mold. To free the part, you must cut through these gates using your nippers. Even with the most careful cutting technique, the act of removing the part leaves a small stress mark or an uneven nub on the plastic. You then need to clean up that nub by shaving it down with a hobby knife and sanding it smooth.

If you have already painted the part on the runner, this necessary cleanup work becomes a disaster. The cutting and sanding will inevitably damage the paint layer around the gate area, leaving a raw, unpainted spot of plastic surrounded by a flaking or chipped ring of paint. You cannot simply touch up that spot, because the sanding has also removed the smooth surface that paint needs to adhere to. Furthermore, the nub mark itself, even after sanding, may still be slightly visible as a discolored spot or a slight depression, and painting over it after the fact rarely matches the surrounding coat perfectly. In essence, painting on the runner guarantees that every single part in your kit will have a visible, unsightly, and difficult-to-repair blemish exactly where it was attached to the frame.

The second, and perhaps even more compelling, reason to avoid painting on the runner has to do with the fundamental workflow of building a seamless model. As discussed in earlier conversations, many Gundam parts are made of two halves that snap together, leaving a visible seam line down the middle. To achieve a professional, realistic look, you need to glue those two halves together with plastic cement, let them fuse, and then sand the seam line away until it disappears completely. This process of sanding removes a thin layer of plastic from the entire surface of the assembled part.

If you had painted the two halves while they were still on the runner, you would face an impossible situation. The moment you glue the halves together, the seam line appears, and you cannot ignore it because it ruins the illusion of a single solid object. But if you then try to sand that seam line away, you will immediately destroy the paint on both halves around the entire joint. You would be left with a beautifully painted part that has a raw, unpainted, sanded seam running right down its center. You would then have to repaint the entire part from scratch, wasting all the effort you put into painting on the runner in the first place.

The correct workflow, therefore, is to postpone all painting until after you have completed the necessary surface preparation. You first cut the parts from the runners, clean up the nub marks, and test-fit them. Then, for parts that have visible seam lines, you glue the two halves together, allow the cement to cure, and sand the seam smooth. Only after this sanding is complete and the part has a perfectly uniform, seamless surface do you apply any primer or paint. This way, your paint goes onto a finished, prepared surface, and you never have to cut, sand, or damage a painted area.

Another practical concern is that Gundam kits often require parts to be assembled in layers. An arm might have an inner frame piece, followed by an outer armor piece that slides over it, followed by a small vent piece that fits into a recess. If you paint parts on the runner, you cannot assemble them to check the fit without risking scratching the paint off the contact points. Paint adds thickness, no matter how thinly you apply it, and that extra thickness can make parts too tight to fit together or, in the case of moving joints, can cause the paint to scrape off as soon as you pose the model.

Furthermore, the simple act of handling parts during assembly will scratch and mar a painted surface. Your fingers, tweezers, and even the edges of other parts will inevitably come into contact with the painted areas as you try to push, snap, and align everything into place. Model paint, especially acrylics, is not nearly as durable as the plastic underneath, and it scratches and chips very easily. If you paint after assembly is complete, you handle the model much less, and you can also use tools like alligator clips on sticks to hold the model by unseen areas, such as the inside of a joint or the back of a shield, where scratches will not matter.

There are a few very narrow exceptions where painting on the runner is acceptable. For example, if you are painting a small, simple part that has no seam lines and attaches to the model by a peg that will be completely hidden, such as a small thruster bell or a sensor lens, you could paint it on the runner and then carefully touch up the nub mark after cutting. Similarly, if you are applying a single uniform color to an entire inner frame and you know that the gate marks will be hidden once the armor is attached, painting on the runner might save time. However, these are advanced shortcuts for experienced builders who understand the risks. For a standard build, and certainly for a first painting project, you should always cut, clean, glue, sand, and then paint. This order of operations is the foundation of professional-looking results and will save you from endless frustration and rework.

An alternative would be to use a clipping system, such as the Mr. Hobby Mr. Almighty Clip II system:

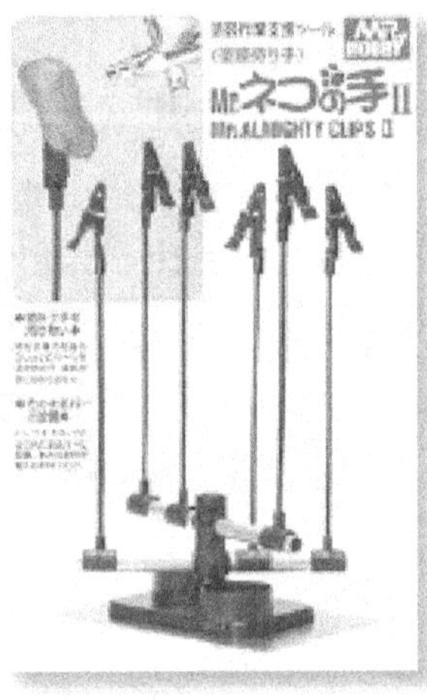

Runner stand and clipping system

A runner stand is genuinely useful for almost any builder. Keeping your runners organized and upright dramatically reduces clutter on your workbench. When runners lie flat, they tend to slide on top of each other, and you waste time constantly moving them around to find the correct one. With a stand, each runner is visible at a glance, and you can simply reach for the one you need without disturbing anything else. This is especially helpful for larger kits with ten or more runners, where managing the mess becomes a significant part of the build challenge. Runner stands are also quite inexpensive, with basic versions costing very little, and some builders even make their own using a block of wood with slots cut into it. For this reason, a runner stand is widely recommended as a worthwhile investment even for beginners.

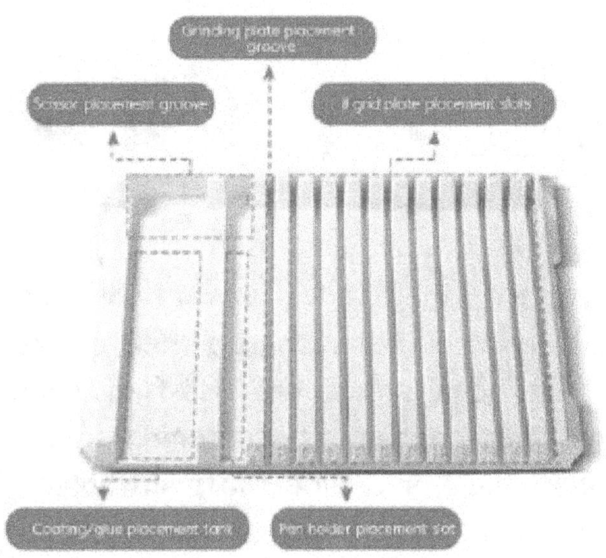

Multifunctional Model Parts Shelf Tool Stan Gundam Model Assembling

★ ★ ★ ★ ★ 4.8 18 Reviews | 84 sold

£ 4.79 35% off £7.37

Price includes VAT

A painting clip system, however, is useful only if you plan to paint your models. For a builder who simply snap-builds their Gunpla and applies panel liners and topcoat without full painting, a clip system is entirely unnecessary. You have no need to hold individual parts in mid-air because you are not spraying them with paint. For a painter, though, a clip system is essential. Without clips, you would have to hold each part in your fingers while spraying, which would lead to uneven coats and paint on your hands. You could lay parts on a piece of cardboard and spray them, but then the side touching the cardboard would remain unpainted, and you would have to flip every part over after the first side dries. This is tedious and risks damaging the dried paint. A clip system allows you to paint every side of a part in a single session, and you can clip dozens of parts at once, making the painting process vastly more efficient.

No tool is without its drawbacks. A runner stand takes up vertical space on your desk, so if you work in a very low-clearance area such as a shelf or under a cabinet, the upright runners might not fit. Some stands are also flimsy and can tip over if you accidentally bump them, sending runners scattering across the floor. A well-designed stand with a heavy base or a wide footprint solves this problem, but cheap stands can be frustrating.

For painting clip systems, the main limitation is that you cannot clip every part easily. Some parts are very small, have no convenient hidden edge to grip, or are shaped in a way that the alligator clip simply cannot hold them securely. For these parts, you may need to use double-sided tape or sticky tack on a stick instead. Additionally, the metal teeth of the alligator clip can scratch the plastic if you are not careful, and if you are painting, the clip itself will leave a small unpainted spot where it gripped the part. You then have to touch that spot up by hand after the part is assembled. Experienced painters accept this as a necessary trade-off, but it is worth knowing before you invest.

Taking care of the small burr

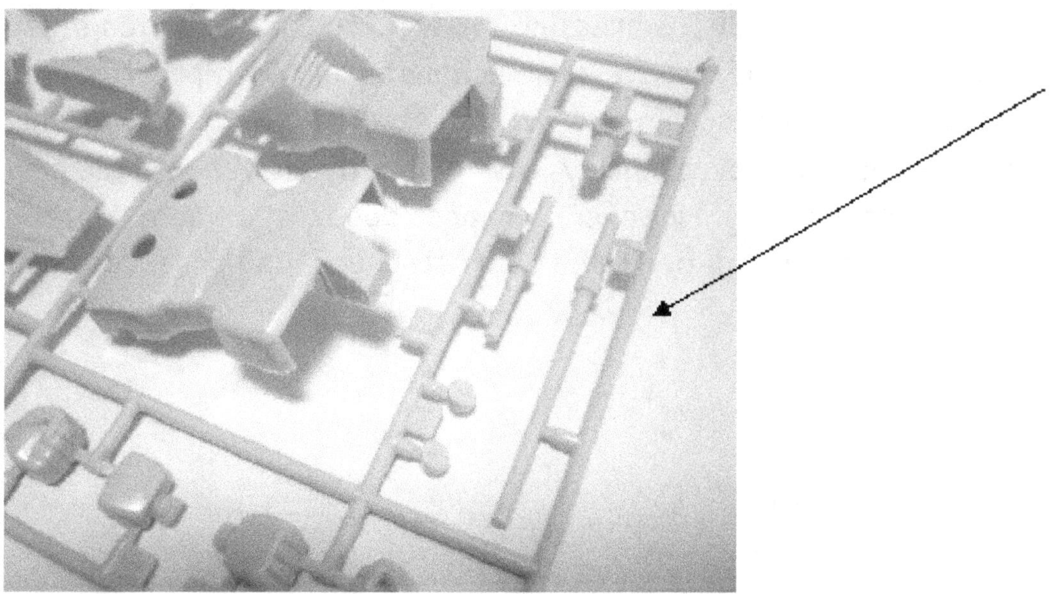

The easiest and most time-efficient method, which requires no sanding at all, is to use a high-quality pair of single-bladed nippers and a two-cut technique. You make your first cut about two to three millimeters away from the part, leaving a small stub of plastic attached. This relieves the stress on the part and prevents the plastic from tearing or turning white. Then, you make a second cut as flush to the part surface as possible using the same nippers. With a premium tool like a GodHand or a Tamiya Sharp Pointed nipper, this second cut can leave a surface that is incredibly smooth, almost as if the part was molded without a gate. The slight remaining burr is often so minimal that it becomes nearly invisible to the naked eye, especially on colored plastic. For many builders, especially those who do not paint their kits, this two-cut method is sufficient. You simply accept that a tiny mark may remain, and you move on, because from a normal viewing distance on a display shelf, it will not be noticeable.

If your nippers are not premium single-bladed tools, or if the second cut leaves a small raised ridge of plastic, the next easiest step is to use a sharp hobby knife. After making your two cuts, you take the knife and gently shave away the remaining burr by running the blade across the surface at a shallow angle, almost parallel to the part. You are not digging into the plastic; you are peeling off thin layers like you are shaving a piece of wood. This method requires a very sharp blade and a light touch, as pressing too hard or cutting at too steep an angle will gouge the plastic or remove too much material. With practice, you can get a very clean, flat surface in just a few seconds per nub. The only difficulty is that the blade can occasionally leave a slightly uneven surface or a small divot if your angle is wrong. However, for most builders, a hobby knife is the standard tool for nub removal because it is fast, cheap, and produces good results.

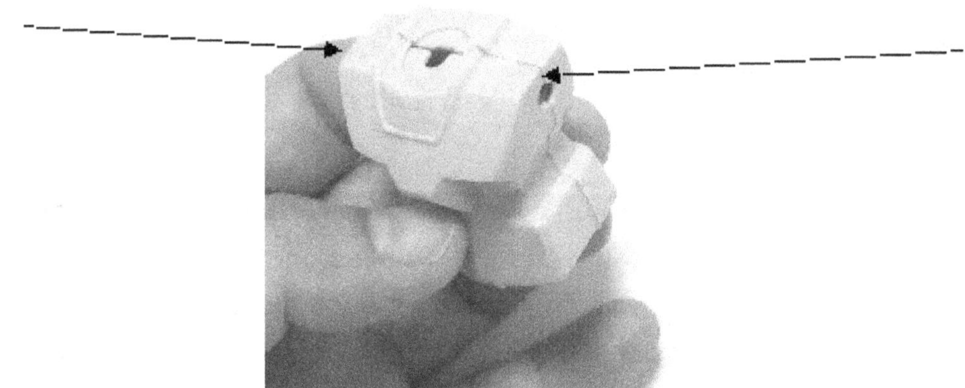

Many beginners are intimidated by sanding, fearing it will take a long time or ruin the part. In reality, sanding a nub mark is one of the easiest and most forgiving techniques once you have the right tool. You simply take a sanding stick or a piece of sandpaper with a medium grit, such as 600 or 800, and rub it back and forth over the nub area a few times. The burr disappears almost instantly. The trick is that sanding leaves fine scratches on the plastic, so if you want the surface to look as glossy and smooth as the rest of the part, you need to follow up with a finer grit, such as 1000 or 1500, to polish those scratches away. However, if you are not concerned about an absolutely perfect mirror finish, a single pass with 800 grit will remove the burr completely, and the slight matte texture it leaves behind is often less noticeable than the original shiny nub mark. Sanding is actually easier than using a hobby knife because there is no risk of cutting yourself or gouging the plastic. You simply rub, and the burr is gone.

The new standard among serious Gunpla builders is the glass file, sometimes called a nano glass file. A good quality glass file, such as the Gunprimer Raser or a generic brand, removes plastic burrs incredibly quickly and leaves behind a polished, glossy surface that matches the original finish of the part. You rub the file over the nub a few times, and the plastic shreds away as a fine white dust, leaving a smooth, shiny surface that requires no further sanding or polishing. The learning curve is minimal, and the results are superior to both knife shaving and traditional sandpaper. The only downsides are that a good glass file costs more than sandpaper or a basic hobby knife, and the tool can become clogged with plastic dust, requiring occasional cleaning with a piece of sticky tape. For many builders, however, the glass file is the easiest method overall because it combines speed, safety, and excellent results in one tool.

And you may have noticed that even after you remove the physical burr, the spot where the nub was can sometimes appear white or darker than the surrounding plastic. This is called a stress mark, and it occurs when the plastic is stretched or compressed during the cutting process. The easiest way to deal with a stress mark is to ignore it if the part is going to be painted, as the primer and paint will cover it completely. If you are not painting, you can often make the white mark disappear by simply rubbing it firmly with your thumbnail. The heat and pressure from your nail can temporarily restore the color. For a more permanent fix, you can apply a tiny drop of plastic cement to the mark, let it dry, and then sand it smooth again. This melts the stressed plastic and allows it to re-form in its original color. However, this takes more time and care, so it is not the easiest method. For most builders, accepting that a small mark may remain on the underside or inside of the part is perfectly fine.

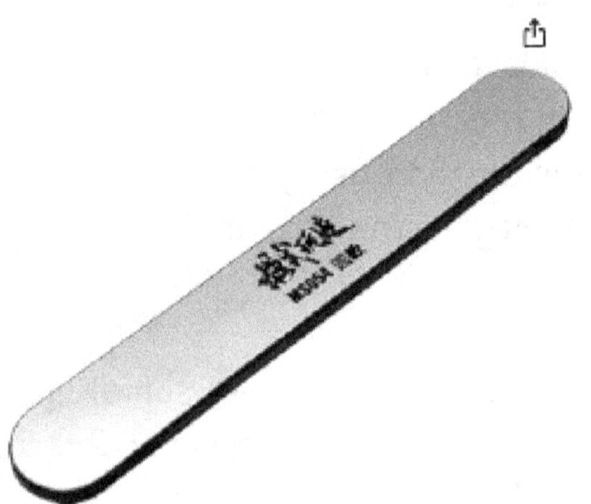

SM SunniMix Precision Glass File for Gundam Mod
Hobby Polishing and for Plane Kits Washable Han

Brand: SM SunniMix

5.0 ★★★★★ ∨ (8)

£6⁴⁹

Save 5% at checkout Qualifying items › | Terms

Save 7% on any 3 Qualifying items › | Terms

Up to 10% off if you qualify Qualifying items › | Terms

Up to 10% off if you qualify Qualifying items › | Terms

Get a £20 Amazon Gift Card if approved for The Amazon Barclaycard. Representative 28.9%
Amazon EU S.A.R.L. Lender: Barclays. T&Cs apply.

- ✔ [Mirror Polished Glass File For Models] A variety of styles are available to mee

If you want the single easiest method that balances cost, speed, and quality, buy a pair of decent single-bladed nippers and learn the two-cut technique. For the small burr that remains, use a glass file OR any plastic modeling file, which will remove it in three seconds and leave a polished surface. This combination is fast enough that it adds almost no time to your build, requires no complicated skill, and produces results that are good enough for even a painted competition model. If you do not want to buy a glass file, a simple sanding stick with 800 grit on one side and 1500 on the other is the next best option and is very inexpensive. The key is to avoid the temptation to simply snap the part off the runner with your hands or to cut it flush in one go with dull nippers. That approach always leaves a jagged, torn burr that is much harder to clean up later. Taking a few seconds per nub to do a proper two-cut removal and a quick sand or file will dramatically improve the appearance of your finished model with very little extra effort.

If none of these are available, a simple nail clipper may help as well :)

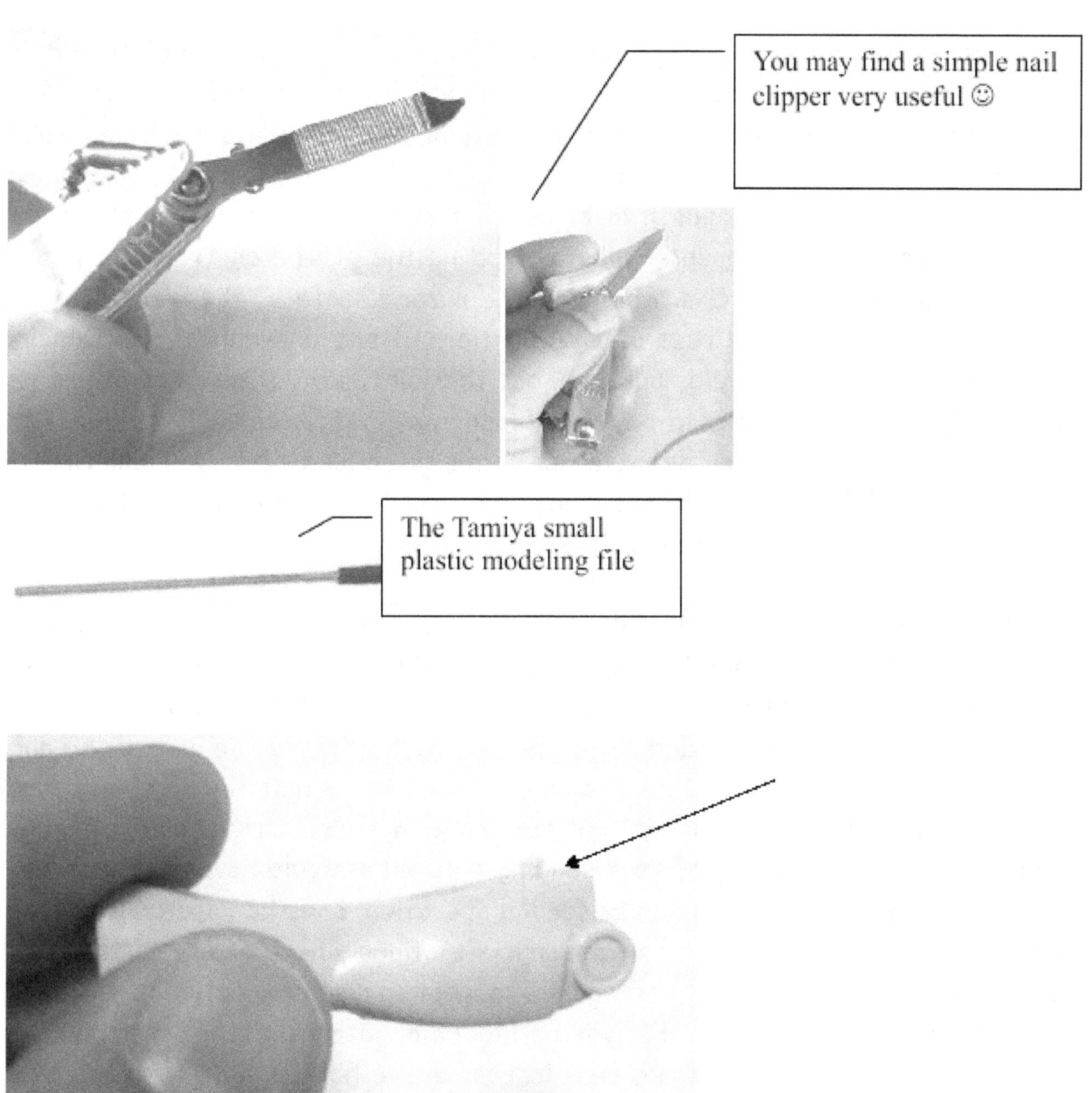

A major reason to remove any burr before gluing is that the burr can prevent the parts from fitting together correctly. When you press two halves of a part together, such as the front and back of a forearm or the left and right halves of a beam rifle, they are designed to meet along a flat, flush seam. If a small raised burr remains on the edge of one part, it will act like a tiny wedge, holding the two surfaces apart. You might still be able to snap the parts together, but the burr will create a small gap on one side while the other side touches perfectly. This results in a visible seam line that is actually wider than it should be. Even worse, the force of snapping the parts together can crush the burr into a flat, deformed lump that is now trapped inside the seam, making it much harder to sand smooth later. Also, glue needs clean, flat surfaces to bond properly. Plastic cement works by melting the plastic and fusing the two pieces together. If there is a burr on the mating surface, the glue will melt that burr along with the rest of the plastic, but the unevenness will remain. The two parts may still weld together, but the joint may not be as strong or as perfectly aligned as it should be. More importantly, if you glue first and then try to sand the burr off the exterior of an assembled part, you will find it much more difficult to reach the small raised area without also sanding away the surrounding surface detail.

Another reason is simple efficiency. It is far easier to remove a burr from a single, flat, loose part than from an assembled three-dimensional object. When the part is still separate, you can lay it flat on your cutting mat, hold it securely with your fingers, and rub a sanding stick or glass file across the nub area with perfect control. Once the part is glued to its matching half, you now have a larger, bulkier assembly that may have awkward curves or protruding details that get in the way of your sanding tool. What could have been a three-second operation becomes a thirty-second operation, and the results are often less clean. Still, there are a few specific situations where removing the burr before gluing is not the best approach. The most common exception is when the burr is located on a surface that will be hidden or internal after assembly. For example, if the burr is on a peg that inserts into a hole, or on the inside of a part that will never be seen once the model is complete, removing the burr is largely unnecessary regardless of when you do it. You could simply glue the parts together and ignore the burr entirely, as it will be trapped inside and invisible. In this case, gluing first and never worrying about the burr at all is perfectly fine.

Another exception involves very small or delicate parts. If a part is tiny and difficult to hold, such as a small sensor lens or a thin fin, you might find it easier to glue it into place first so that you have a larger assembly to grip while you carefully remove the burr. However, you must be extremely cautious with this approach, because slipping with your knife or sanding stick after assembly could damage not only the part you are working on but also the adjacent parts that are already glued in place. For most builders, it is safer to struggle with holding the small part before gluing than to risk ruining an entire assembly.

My personal preference is to first take care of it prior to gluing. After the parts are glued together, the next thing to do is to fill the gaps with putty and finally sanding.

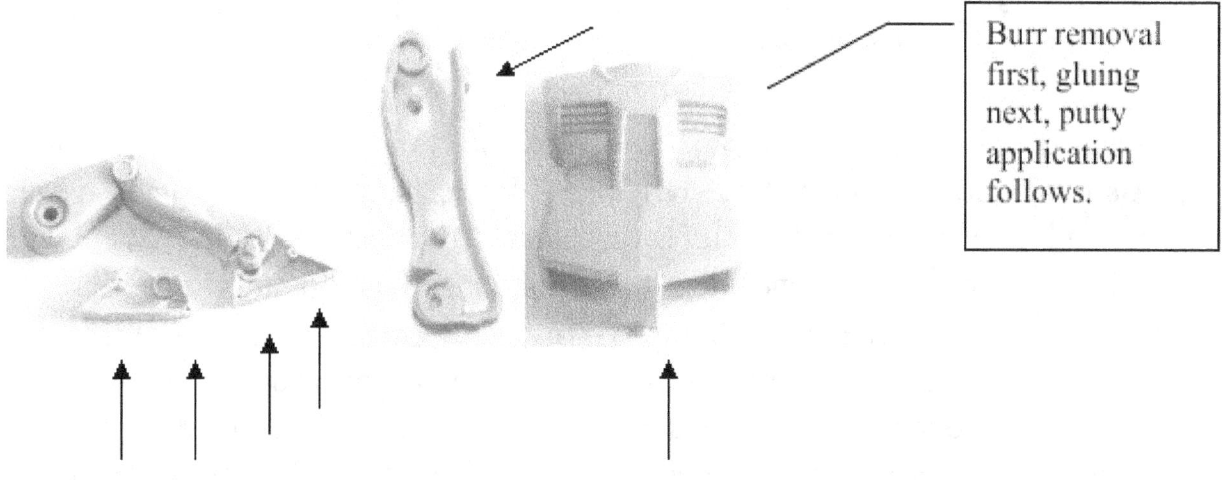

Dry fitting

Dry fitting means assembling the parts exactly as the instruction manual shows, but without using any glue or cement. You press the pieces together firmly enough that they hold their shape, but not so hard that they become permanently locked or difficult to separate. For snap-fit Gundam kits, this is very easy, as the parts are designed to click together and can usually be pulled apart with gentle pressure. For older kits or non-Bandai models that require glue, you simply hold the parts in place with your fingers or use a piece of removable tape to keep them aligned. The goal is to see how the parts interact when they are in their final positions, but without committing to a permanent bond.

The first and most obvious reason to dry fit is to confirm that you have the correct parts and the correct orientation. Instruction manuals are generally clear, but mistakes happen. You might misread a part number, or you might accidentally pick up a similar-looking piece from a different runner. You might also try to assemble a part backwards or upside down. If you glue first and then realize your error, you are facing a difficult and often destructive process of prying the parts apart, cleaning off the dried glue, and starting over. If you dry fit first, you discover the mistake immediately, and the only consequence is a few seconds of lost time. You simply separate the parts, find the correct ones, and try again.

The second reason is to check the quality of the fit. Even with modern, precision-engineered Bandai kits, not every fit is perfect. Sometimes a part has a small burr or a speck of leftover plastic that prevents the two halves from closing completely. Sometimes the design itself has a slight gap that will need to be filled with putty. By dry fitting, you can see exactly where the parts touch, where they do not, and how much of a gap you are dealing with. You can then address these issues before the glue is applied, whether that means sanding down a burr, shaving off a tiny bit of plastic, or preparing to apply putty to a known gap. Trying to fix a poor fit after the glue has already set is much more difficult and often results in a messy, uneven seam.

Finally, dry fitting allows you to see exactly where the seam line will be and how pronounced it is. You can also test whether the two halves align perfectly or if one side is slightly taller than the other. This information tells you how much putty you will need and where you will need to focus your sanding effort. If you skip dry fitting and go straight to gluing, you might be surprised to find a step or a mismatched edge that requires extensive putty work, and you may have already glued the parts in a way that makes that putty work more difficult than it needed to be.

When you dry fit a pair of parts, you should examine a few specific things.

First, check that the edges meet flush along the entire seam. If you see a gap, try pressing harder to see if it closes. If it does not close, look for a burr, a piece of debris, or a molding imperfection that is holding the parts apart. Second, check the alignment of surface details. Panel lines should continue smoothly from one half to the other. If they do not match up, the parts may be warped or you may have the wrong halves paired together. Third, check for any interference or binding. If the parts are supposed to move freely after assembly, such as a joint or a sliding mechanism, dry fitting allows you to test that motion before any glue permanently locks it in place. Fourth, check the overall shape and symmetry. Does the assembled part look correct? Does it match the diagram in the manual? If something looks off, trust your eyes and investigate before you commit to glue.

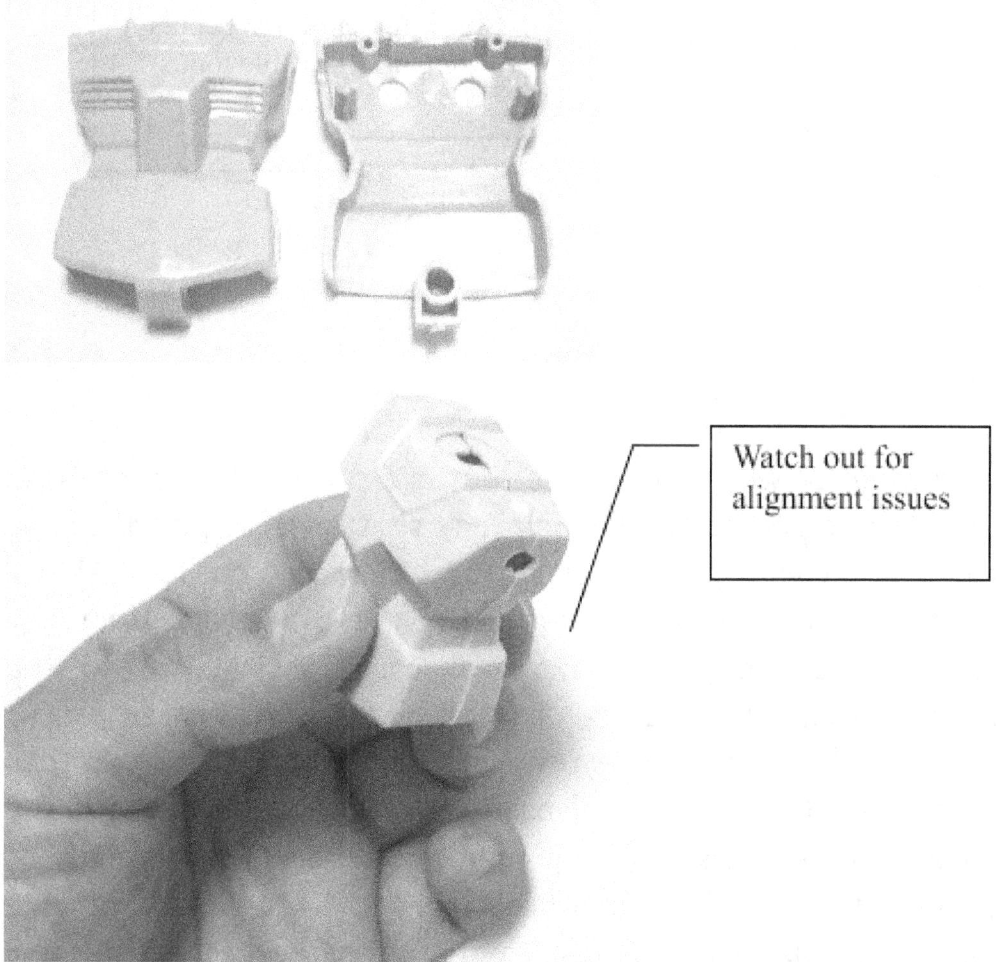

Alignment issues

The plastic can deform during and after the manufacturing process.

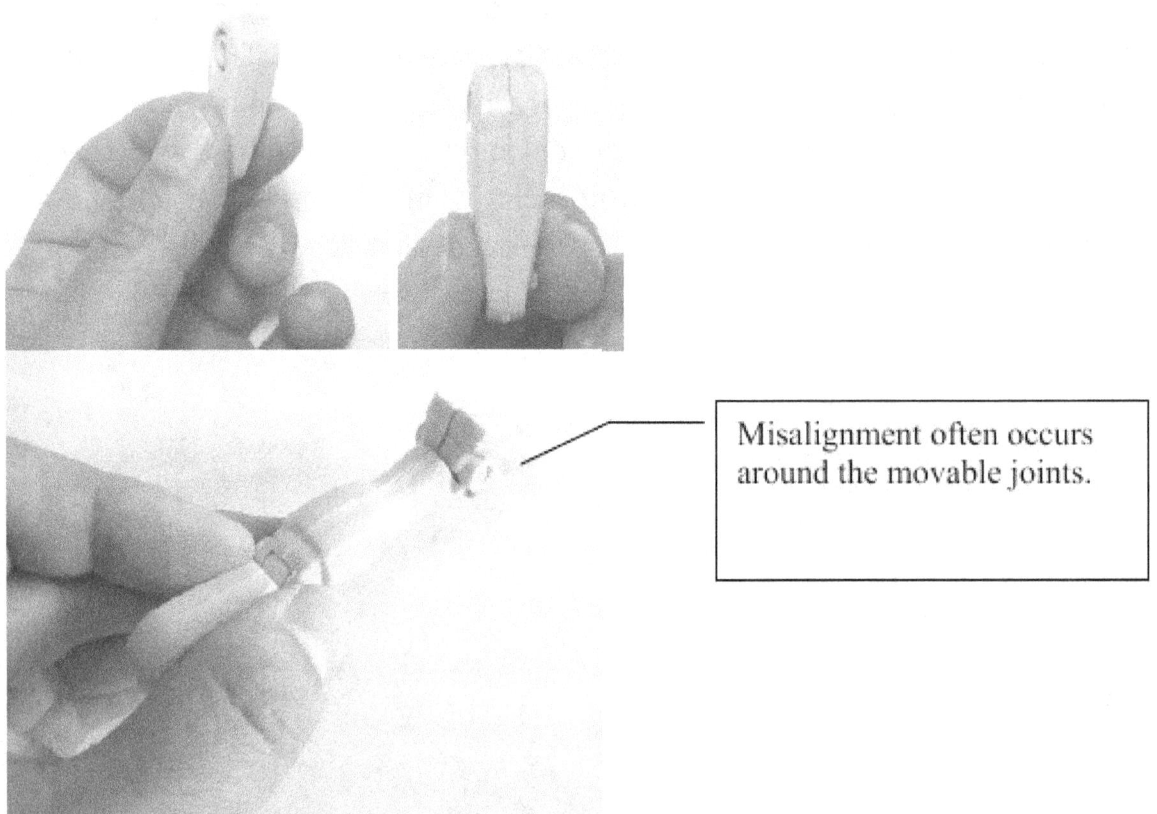

Parts alignment issues occur when two pieces that are supposed to meet flush along a seam do not line up perfectly. One half may sit slightly higher than the other, or there may be a gap at one end while the other end touches. Several factors cause these problems, ranging from the way the kit was manufactured to the way you prepared the parts. The first cause is inherent to the manufacturing process. Gundam parts are created by injecting molten plastic into steel molds. Each mold is made of two or more halves that clamp together with extreme precision. If the mold halves are not perfectly aligned, the resulting plastic part will have a slight step or mismatch along the line where the mold halves meet. This is called mold misalignment. On a well-maintained mold, this step is microscopic and invisible to the naked eye. However, as a mold ages and goes through thousands of injection cycles, the steel can wear down slightly, and the clamping mechanism can develop tiny amounts of play. When this happens, the parts produced later in the mold's life may have small but visible alignment issues. This is why very old kits or kits that have been reprinted many times are more likely to have fit problems than brand new, first-run kits.

A second and very common cause is plastic shrinkage. When molten plastic is injected into a mold, it is hot and under pressure. As it cools, it contracts. The plastic near the gate, which is the small opening where the plastic enters the mold cavity, cools differently from the plastic at the far end of the part. This differential cooling can cause the part to warp or shrink unevenly. If a part has large gates attached to one side, that side may cool and contract in a way that pulls the part slightly out of its intended shape. When you then try to fit that slightly warped part against its perfectly flat counterpart, you will see alignment problems. This is one reason why premium kits use multiple small gates rather than one large gate, as smaller gates reduce uneven shrinkage.

The third cause is the one you have the most control over, and it is also the most common: improper nub removal. As discussed in earlier conversations, every part has small nubs where it was attached to the runner. If you cut flush with your nippers in a single cut, you can leave a compressed or torn burr that sits above the surface of the part. If you leave this burr on the mating edge of a part, it will act as a tiny spacer, preventing the two halves from closing completely. One side of the seam may touch perfectly, but the side with the burr will have a gap or will push the part out of alignment, causing a step. Similarly, if you shave too aggressively with a hobby knife and accidentally remove more plastic than intended, you can create a depression on the mating surface. The adjacent part will then rock or tilt into that depression, creating a misalignment at the opposite end of the seam.

Plastic is not perfectly rigid, especially on thin or long parts. A beam rifle barrel, a long skirt armor piece, or a large shield can warp over time if stored improperly, such as being left in a hot car, placed under heavy objects, or exposed to direct sunlight. Even the pressure of being packed tightly in a box for years can cause some parts to develop a slight curve. When you try to glue a warped part to a straight part, the warped one will resist lying flat. You may be able to force it into alignment with clamps or rubber bands while the glue dries, but the internal stress remains, and the part may eventually pull itself out of alignment or crack along the seam.

Sometimes the alignment issue is not with the parts themselves but with how you are assembling them. For example, a leg assembly might require you to insert an inner frame piece between two armor halves before closing the seam. If you snap the armor halves together first and then try to force the inner frame piece inside, the pressure from the inner frame can push the armor halves apart or twist them out of alignment. The correct sequence, as shown in the instruction manual, is to lay the inner frame piece into one armor half, then place the other armor half on top and press evenly. Similarly, if you apply glue unevenly or use too much glue, the solvent can temporarily soften the plastic, allowing it to distort under its own weight or under the pressure of your fingers. When the glue dries, the part may have cured in a slightly twisted or misaligned position.

This is precisely why dry fitting is so important.

Sub-assembly

When you build the entire model according to the instruction manual, snapping every part into its final position, you end up with a complete, poseable figure. This is satisfying to see, but it creates several problems for finishing work. First, many parts become inaccessible. Seams that are buried between an arm and a torso, or hidden behind a weapon held in two hands, become impossible to reach with sandpaper or a putty applicator. Second, moving joints and overlapping armor pieces create what painters call "shadow zones," where spray paint cannot reach because other parts block the angle. Third, you cannot paint subassemblies separately because they are already locked together. A leg that is permanently attached to a hip joint cannot be removed for painting without risking breakage. Fourth, and most frustratingly, you will inevitably handle the model to reach different areas, and your fingers will rub against painted surfaces, leaving fingerprints, smudges, or even rubbing the paint off entirely.

Sub-assembly means building the model in large, logical chunks that are not yet connected to each other. Instead of assembling the entire mecha, you assemble the head completely, then the torso completely, then the left arm completely, then the right arm completely, then the waist completely, and then each leg completely. You stop at this point. The head is not attached to the torso. The arms and legs are not attached to the torso. The weapons are built separately. You now have a collection of completed sub-assemblies, each of which is a finished unit ready for putty, sanding, painting, and decals.

Putty is used to fill gaps and eliminate seam lines. When you work in sub-assemblies, every seam on every part of the model is fully accessible. You can glue the two halves of a forearm together, let the cement cure, apply putty to the seam if needed, and sand the entire surface smooth from every angle, because the forearm is a loose piece sitting on your workbench. You can rotate it, hold it in your hand, or clamp it to a stand. There is no torso blocking the elbow end, and no hand attachment getting in the way of your sanding stick. Once the forearm is perfectly seamless, you set it aside and move to the next sub-assembly. By the time you have finished all the sub-assemblies, every seam on the entire model has been addressed, and no seam is left hidden or inaccessible.

Painting also becomes dramatically easier with sub-assemblies. Each sub-assembly is a manageable size that you can hold with a handle or mount on a painting stand. You can spray each sub-assembly from every angle because there are no other parts blocking the way. The head can be painted completely, including the underside of the chin and the back of the neck, because the torso is not attached. The inside of a shield can be painted as easily as the front, because the shield is not attached to the arm. Most importantly, you can paint parts that have different colors separately and then assemble them afterwards. For example, you can paint the white armor pieces of a leg separately from the grey inner frame, then snap them together after the paint has cured, achieving perfect color separation without any masking tape.

The correct workflow for a painted build is different from a snap-build. First, you cut all parts from the runners, clean up the nub marks, and perform any necessary sanding or putty work on individual parts. Second, you identify which parts need to be glued together to eliminate seam lines, such as the two halves of a forearm or the two halves of a rifle. You glue these parts together, fill the seams with putty if needed, and sand them smooth. You now have a solid sub-assembly, such as a complete forearm or a complete rifle. Third, you prime and paint each sub-assembly separately, using masking tape if a single sub-assembly has multiple colors. Fourth, after the paint has fully cured, you assemble the sub-assemblies into the final model. The head snaps onto the torso, the arms snap onto the shoulders, the legs snap onto the hips, and the weapons are placed into the hands. Because you left moving joints and connection points unpainted or carefully masked, everything fits together without scratching or binding.

Polycaps are the soft, rubbery joint pieces that allow your Gundam to move. These present a special challenge because paint does not adhere well to them and will scrape off if the joint is moved. The solution is to not paint polycaps at all. Leave them raw. When you are painting a sub-assembly that contains a polycap, you either remove the polycap before painting or mask it off with a small piece of tape. For example, a shoulder joint may have a polycap that the arm peg inserts into. You would paint the shoulder sub-assembly with the polycap removed, then snap the polycap back into place after the paint is dry. For moving joints that are not polycaps, such as a peg sliding into a socket, you should mask the contact surfaces or simply leave them unpainted, as the friction of movement will scrape any paint off anyway.

There is one scenario where full assembly before finishing is actually better, and that is when you are not painting or applying putty at all. For a straight snap-build where you simply want to panel line and topcoat the model, assembling everything first is perfectly fine. The small seam lines that remain are acceptable at that level of finish, and topcoat can be sprayed over the fully assembled model without difficulty. However, once you decide to use putty to eliminate seams or paint to change colors, sub-assembly becomes the correct and necessary approach.

It is often easier to process the individual body components (arms, legs, head …etc) first prior to putting them together. The thing is, the original joint scheme may make it difficult for you to work on a component-by- component basis. For example, the head must be inserted into the body before you can close up the body. One thing you can do is to abandon the original joint. For example:

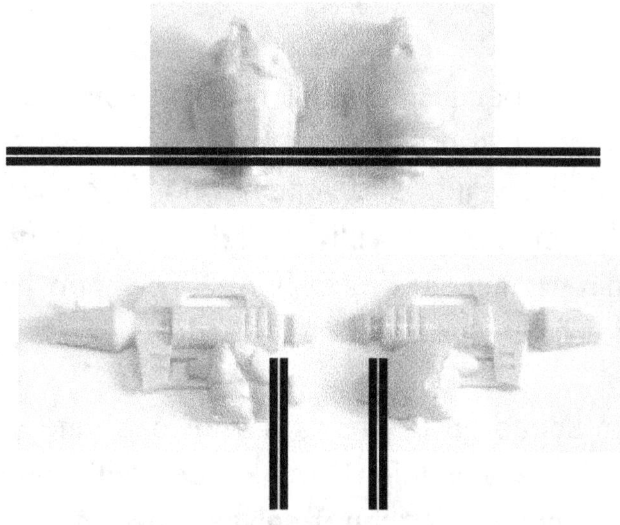

However, not all joints can be easily abandoned:

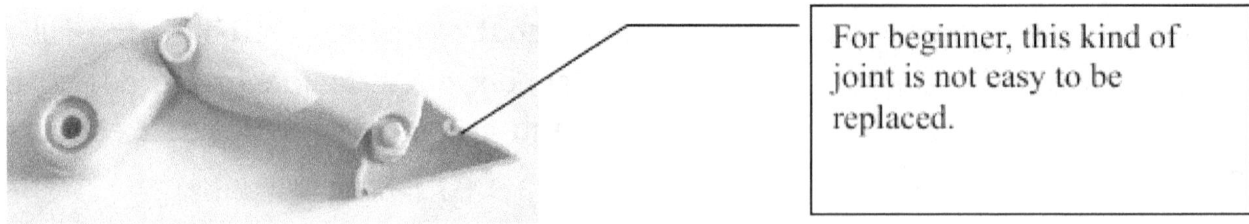

We recommend that you use a low cost model kit to experiment with. After all, joint re-design is never easy!

The curing process

The curing process for plastic cement has two distinct stages, and understanding these will help you plan your workflow. The first stage is the set time, which is when the glue has hardened enough that the parts will stay together on their own; for thin liquid cements like Tamiya Extra Thin, this takes about five to ten minutes, while for standard tube cements, it can be as quick as one to two minutes. The second stage is the full cure time, which is when the chemical reaction is complete and the plastic has fully re-solidified to its maximum strength, and for both types of cement this takes approximately twenty-four hours.

Waiting is non-negotiable because plastic cement works by chemically melting the plastic to fuse parts into a single piece. If you stress the bond before it has set, the pieces will likely just slide apart, and if you sand or apply pressure to a part that is only set but not fully cured, the softened plastic can warp, deform, or even retain permanent fingerprints. The joint will also be weaker in the long run if it is not given the full time to solidify.

Using a hair dryer to speed up drying is a bad idea, and you should avoid any direct heat source. While you might think heat will evaporate the solvents faster, it creates more problems than it solves. The plastic cement softens the material at a microscopic level so the pieces can weld together, and adding intense, uneven heat from a hair dryer can easily cause the part to warp, bend, or lose its shape entirely. Rapidly evaporating the solvents can also create tiny bubbles within the still-soft plastic, leading to a brittle and ugly joint. Furthermore, it is surprisingly easy to get a hair dryer too close to a model piece and accidentally melt delicate details like fins or antennas. Instead of heat, patience is the real secret ingredient.

If you are in a hurry, there are safe accelerators designed specifically to speed up the curing of super glue and, to a lesser extent, plastic cement. For super glue, which you might use for attaching metal parts or different materials, you can use a CA accelerator, sometimes called a kicker. You spray a tiny amount onto the glued joint, and it cures the super glue almost instantly within seconds. However, you should use this very sparingly on Gunpla, as some accelerators can leave a white, chalky residue on the surrounding plastic. It is best to spray some into a disposable cup and apply it with a fine brush for pinpoint accuracy.

For plastic cement itself, there are specialized products such as the DSPIAE BP-A Coagulation Accelerator, which is formulated to speed up the reaction of solvent-based cements and putties. Even with these products, you must always work in a well-ventilated area, as the fumes from accelerators mixed with cement can be very strong.

Often, simply working in a room with a fan or an open window is the most effective way to encourage the solvents to evaporate at a natural, safe rate. Your best bet for a healthy, strong model is to simply wait the twenty-four hours, but if you are working with super glue for small metal parts, a CA accelerator is a safe timesaver as long as you are careful. A hair dryer is just not worth the risk.

A fancier option is to use the Mr. Hobby Dry Booth. It is electric powered and can set the temperature to 40C for speeding up the drying process (40C is reasonable). Professional modelers like to use it to dry paints and alike. Mioromark has a similar offering.

Regarding options for holding them together while the glue dries, the most common and versatile tool is masking tape or painter's tape. Low-tack tapes like Tamiya tape are ideal because they hold firmly but peel off easily without damaging paint or plastic. You can tear off small strips to pull seams together or wrap tape completely around a joint. Standard masking tape works as well, though it has stronger adhesion, so it is best used on bare plastic rather than over delicate painted finishes. Rubber bands are another excellent choice, especially for cylindrical or irregular shapes where tape might not pull evenly. You can loop rubber bands around a fuselage, a fuel tank, or any assembled part that has a natural groove or recess to keep the band from slipping off. For smaller parts, fine elastic thread or even a stretched-out piece of household string can apply gentle, constant tension. Zip ties can sometimes do the trick too.

Spring clamps and clothespins are very useful for larger assemblies or flat joints like wing halves or fuselage seams. However, the jaws of most clamps are quite strong, so you should always pad them with pieces of foam, felt, or folded paper to distribute the pressure and prevent denting the plastic. For very small or delicate parts, you can use locking tweezers or hemostats with padded tips.

For odd shapes or areas where tape and clamps cannot reach easily, you can use Blue-Tack or reusable mounting putty. A small ball pressed between two surfaces will hold them in alignment without sliding, and it leaves no residue. Another simple method is to prop weighted objects against the assembly, such as a small metal ruler, a battery, or even a heavy coin, to provide steady downward pressure while the glue cures. If you are using a fast-setting glue like super glue or five-minute epoxy, you may not need any external clamping at all, because these adhesives develop strength within seconds or minutes. Simply holding the parts together by hand for thirty to sixty seconds is often sufficient. For slower glues like white glue, plastic cement, or slower epoxies, you will likely need to leave the clamps or tape in place for several hours or overnight to ensure a full cure.

The most important principle regardless of the part is to use only enough force to close the seam. Over-tightening with rubber bands or clamps can actually bow the parts out of shape or squeeze all the glue out of the joint, leaving a weak bond. A gentle, even pressure that brings the two surfaces into contact is all that is required.

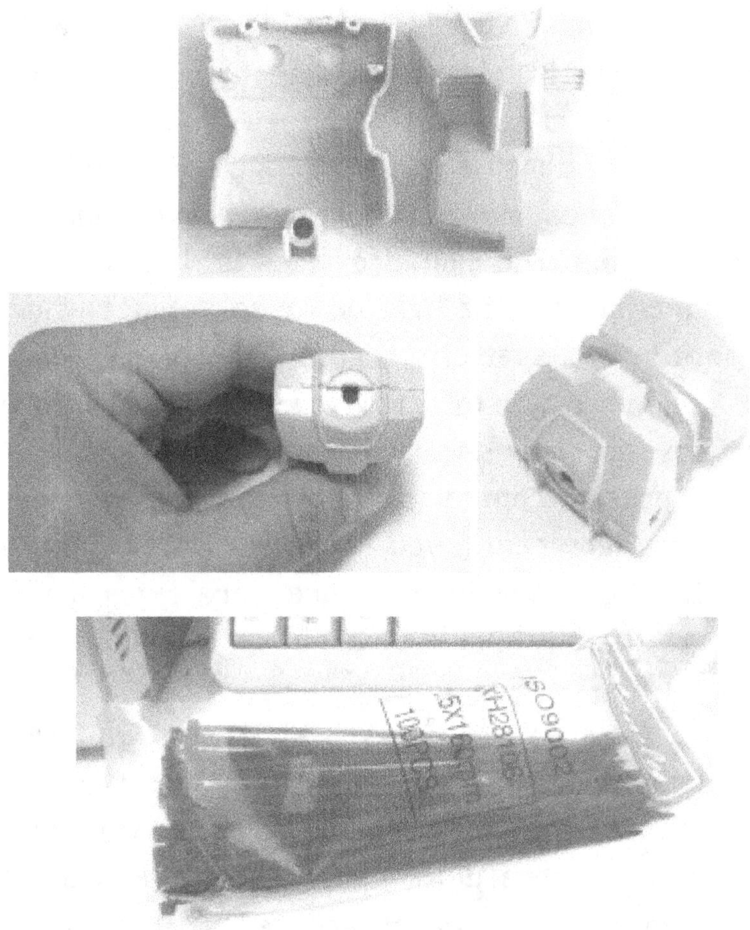

Do not use adhesive tape. Adhesive tape is no good for the plastic surface (it makes the surface very sticky).

Very importantly, before sanding you must wait until the glue/cement is truly cured. Most cements can get dried up in minutes. However, it can take them 12 hours or so to cure. You just have to be patient.

Gluing clear parts

For gluing clear parts like canopies and windows on model kits, the most important rule is to avoid standard super glue and most plastic cements, as the fumes from these will create a permanent, unsightly fogging effect on the clear plastic. The safest and most effective adhesives are water-based white glues or special non-fogging clear formulas.

PVA or white glue, such as Elmer's or Mod Podge, is a good choice because it dries completely clear, is one hundred percent safe to use on clear parts, and is both cheap and easy to find. The main drawback is that it dries slowly and has low initial grip, so parts need to be held or taped in place while the glue sets. For a slightly stronger bond, specialty canopy glues like Revell Contacta Clear, Humbrol Clearfix, or Micro Kristal Klear are specifically designed for this purpose. They dry crystal clear and most include a fine applicator such as a brush or needle for precise control. If you need the strongest and fastest bond that will not fog clear parts, you can use a non-fogging super glue like Madworks or Wiko 1000 UF, though these are more expensive and any spillage is very hard to remove, so they should be applied extremely sparingly.

For the best results, use a wooden cocktail stick or toothpick to apply just a tiny drop of glue to the edge of the clear part, rather than directly onto the transparent surface where it might squeeze out. Even when using non-fogging super glues, it is wise to be careful with vapors, as standard super glue should be kept far away from your work area because the invisible fumes alone can haze clear plastic from across the desk. If you want your clear parts to look extra glossy and realistic, you can dip them in Future Floor Polish or another acrylic floor gloss after gluing, as this fills in micro-scratches and makes the part appear like new glass. In short, the best choice for most modelers is a dedicated clear parts glue or standard PVA glue because they are simple, safe, and inexpensive. The most important takeaway is to keep traditional super glue and plastic cement far away from your clear parts.

The Humbrol Clearfix is a solvent based polymer solution that can be used as an adhesive on clear plastic parts.

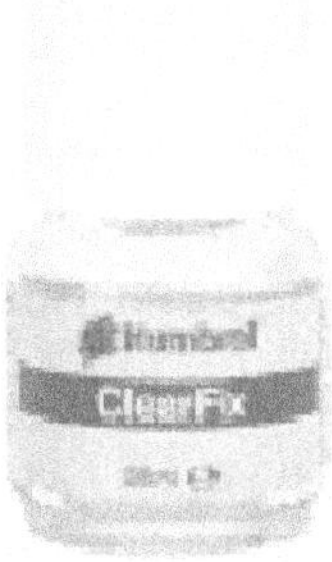

You can use a brush to apply glue for clear parts, but with a few important caveats. A brush can be an excellent tool for applying certain types of glue, particularly PVA or specialty canopy glues, because it allows for very fine control and helps you deposit a thin, even layer exactly where you need it.

If you are using a water-based glue like white glue or a dedicated clear parts glue, a small, fine-tipped brush works wonderfully. You can dip the brush into the glue and then touch it to the edge of the clear part, allowing the glue to wick into the joint by capillary action. This method helps prevent excess glue from squeezing out onto the transparent surface. Just be sure to clean the brush thoroughly with water immediately after use, as dried PVA glue can ruin the bristles.

However, you should never use a good brush with super glue, even the non-fogging variety. Super glue cures almost instantly and will ruin the brush fibers permanently, turning them stiff and brittle. If you need to apply super glue to a clear part, it is better to use a disposable applicator like a toothpick, a piece of thin wire, or the tip of a sewing pin.

One final tip is to keep a dedicated brush just for glue, separate from your painting brushes. Even with water-based glues, it is very difficult to remove every trace of glue from a brush, and any residue left behind could affect future paint work or cause clouding on clear parts if used interchangeably. A cheap, inexpensive brush from a craft store is perfectly suitable for glue application.

Putty application

Overusing putty is a very common experience in modeling, and fortunately it is easy to fix. If you have applied too much putty, the simplest solution is to wait for it to fully cure and then sand it back. Most modeling putties harden within thirty minutes to a few hours, and once dry, you can use fine-grit sandpaper, starting around 320 or 400 grit and working up to 600 or 800 grit, to remove the excess. You want to sand until the putty is flush with the surrounding plastic surface, leaving only what has filled the seam or gap. A sanding stick or flexible sanding sponge is helpful for reaching tight corners or curved areas without flattening detail.

If the putty is still wet or tacky, you can sometimes scrape away the excess with a cocktail stick, an old hobby knife blade, or a small metal spatula before it hardens. This saves you sanding time and reduces dust. Just be gentle so you do not gouge the plastic underneath.

Dark gray putty works perfectly well and has no effect on the strength or adhesion of the joint. However, it can be more difficult to see against dark colored plastics, making it tricky to tell when you have sanded flush. Against light gray, white, or tan plastic, dark gray putty provides excellent contrast, which actually helps you see exactly where the putty remains and where you have reached the bare plastic. The main challenge arises when you are priming or painting. Dark gray putty may show through lighter colored primers or thin paint coats, requiring an extra layer or two to fully cover. If you are painting the finished model a light color such as white, yellow, or light gray, you might prefer a white or light gray putty to minimize the number of primer coats needed. For dark colors like navy blue, olive drab, or black, dark gray putty is perfectly fine and will cover easily.

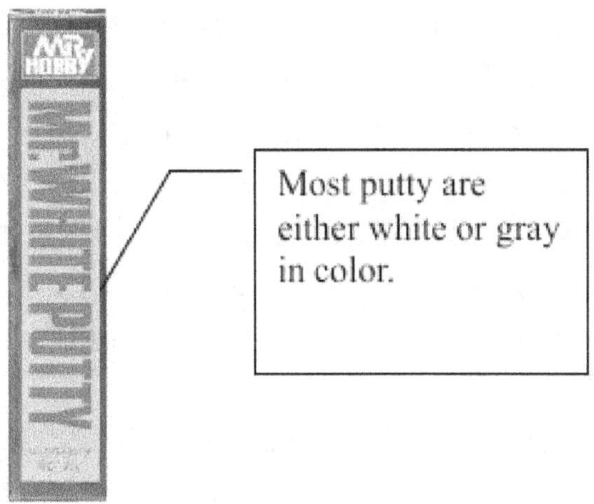

If you are going to sand and paint, in theory the color doesn't really matter.

Different Gundam models have different default colors. Some kits are white out of the box while some are dark gray. You may choose your putty accordingly. Even though your paint is supposed to cover everything, using light color paint to cover darker putty is not easy.

Filling small, difficult-to-reach areas with putty is a common challenge in modeling, but there are several effective techniques you can use to make the job easier and cleaner. The first and most helpful method is to thin your putty so it becomes more fluid and self-levelling. Most standard modeling putties, such as Tamiya Basic Type or Squadron Green Putty, can be thinned with Lacquer Thinner or a dedicated putty thinner. You mix a small amount of putty with a few drops of thinner on a scrap piece of plastic or a metal palette until it reaches a consistency similar to heavy cream or thick paint. This thinned putty can then be applied with a fine brush, allowing it to flow into a tiny seam, pinhole, or recess that you could never reach with a putty knife or your finger. The thinner evaporates quickly, leaving the putty behind in exactly the place you want it. Just be sure to clean your brush immediately with thinner afterward.

For extremely small imperfections like pinprick air bubbles or micro-scratches, you can use a liquid or paste filler rather than a traditional thick putty. Products like Mr. Dissolved Putty or Mr. Surfacer 500 are specifically designed for this purpose and come in bottles with brush applicators. You simply brush them directly into the problem area, let them dry, and then sand or wipe away the excess with a cloth dampened with thinner. These products shrink very little and are ideal for delicate or detailed surfaces where you do not want to risk damaging surrounding raised details.

Another technique for reaching tight corners or recessed areas is to apply the putty using improvised tools rather than your standard putty knife. A cocktail stick or toothpick works wonderfully because it has a fine point and a small wooden surface that can push putty into narrow gaps. You can also flatten the end of a piece of soft wire or use the tip of a sewing pin. For extremely fine work, a silicone shaper or a stiff paintbrush with the bristles cut short can manipulate the putty into place without scratching the plastic.

If the area is difficult to reach because it is surrounded by raised details or delicate features that you do not want to sand later, you can use a technique called "wiping" rather than sanding. After applying the putty and allowing it to partially cure but not fully harden, you take a cotton swab or a soft cloth dampened with a small amount of thinner or acetone and gently wipe away the excess putty. This removes the putty from the surrounding surface while leaving it in the recess or seam where it is needed. This method completely eliminates the need for sanding in that area and preserves all the adjacent detail.

Finally, for the smallest possible repairs, such as a single pinhole or a hairline crack, you can use super glue as a filler instead of putty. A tiny drop of thin super glue applied with the tip of a pin will wick into the gap, and you can then spray it with an accelerator or simply let it cure. Once hard, you can scrape away any excess with the back of a hobby knife blade without needing to sand a broad area. This is particularly useful for areas where a sanding stick would never fit.

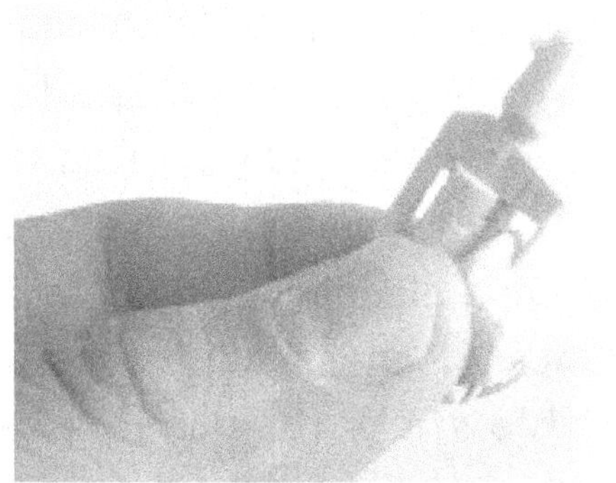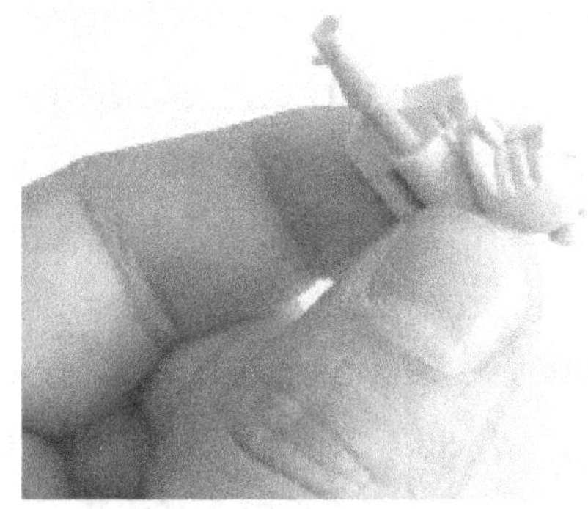

Hard to reach areas are best to be taken care of with thin-down putty.

You need to make the putty as thin as possible. To do this, you can mix acetone (you can find it in nail polish remover) and putty together, then paint the mix on the desired area as needed. Do this with a small paint brush. You may also use the ready-made Mr. Dissolved Putty from Mr. Hobby so no by-hand-mixing is necessary.

Most putty when dried will shrink and crack. Therefore, it is not uncommon for professional modelers to apply TWO or more thin layers of putty on the same area. **The larger the gap, the more layers of putty you are going to need.**

Using masking tape

When you are working with putty, sanding, or painting, you will often want to mask off certain areas to keep them clean or to protect existing paintwork. Masking tape is the perfect tool for this, but choosing the right tape and using it correctly makes all the difference between a professional result and a ruined model. The reason you should choose a good masking tape from a reputable source is that not all tapes are created equal. High-quality hobby masking tapes, such as those made by Tamiya, Aizu, or FrogTape for delicate surfaces, are specifically engineered with low-tack adhesives. This means they stick well enough to stay in place and prevent paint bleed or putty from creeping underneath, but they release easily and cleanly when you are finished. Reputable brands also use adhesives that do not chemically react with model paints or plastics, so you will not end up with a sticky residue left behind or a discolored surface after the tape is removed.

The warning about tape that is too strong tearing off existing paint is a very real and frustrating problem. Standard hardware store masking tape, often beige or tan in color, is designed for painting walls and trim in a house. It has a much stronger adhesive because it needs to stick to rough drywall and stay put for days or weeks. If you use this type of tape on a model, the adhesive can bond so strongly to your painted surface that when you pull the tape off, it lifts the paint right off the plastic, often taking chips of primer and color coats with it. This is especially likely if your paint has not had plenty of time to fully cure, or if you applied it in thin layers that did not bond aggressively to the plastic. The result is a ruined paint job that requires stripping and starting over.

Even some tapes sold in craft stores can be problematic. General-purpose masking tapes or washi tapes may have unpredictable adhesive strength, and some leave a sticky residue that attracts dust and is difficult to remove without using harsh solvents that might damage the paint. Cheap no-name tapes from discount retailers are particularly risky because their adhesive formulas are not consistent, and you have no way of knowing whether they will behave gently or aggressively. To avoid these problems, stick with tape brands that are trusted within the modeling community.

Tamiya masking tape is the gold standard for good reason. It comes in various widths, it is thinly flexible so it conforms to curved surfaces without wrinkling, and its adhesive is strong enough to hold but weak enough to peel off easily without lifting paint. Aizu tape is another excellent Japanese brand with very similar properties. For larger areas or for masking over delicate finishes like pastels or chalk weathering, you can also use painter's tape labeled for delicate surfaces, such as the purple or blue varieties from FrogTape or Scotch Delicate Surface painter's tape.

Before applying any masking tape to a painted model, it is wise to perform a simple test. Apply a small strip of the tape to an inconspicuous area, such as the underside of a wing or inside a fuselage half, and press it down firmly. Leave it for about ten minutes, then peel it off. If the paint remains intact and no residue is left behind, the tape is safe to use on that particular paint finish.

If you are working with a paint that is known to be fragile, such as some acrylics or hand-brushed enamels, you can further reduce the risk by first pressing the tape against your palm or a clean piece of glass a few times. This transfers some of the adhesive away from the tape, lowering its tack before you put it on the model.

When it is time to remove the masking tape, do not simply rip it off like a bandage. Instead, peel it back slowly at a shallow angle, pulling the tape parallel to the surface rather than lifting it straight up. This gentler method reduces the stress on the paint layer. If you feel any resistance, stop and use the tip of a hobby knife to help lift an edge, or warm the tape slightly with a hairdryer on a low setting to soften the adhesive.

There are masking tapes of different widths available, and there are some specially for curves:

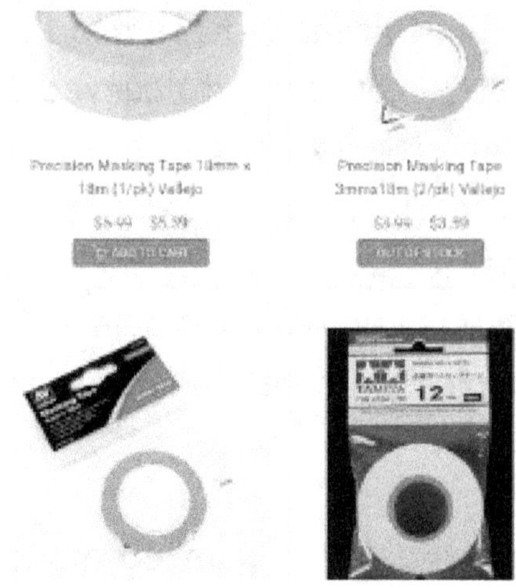

Sanding clear parts

Only higher grade models have clear parts.

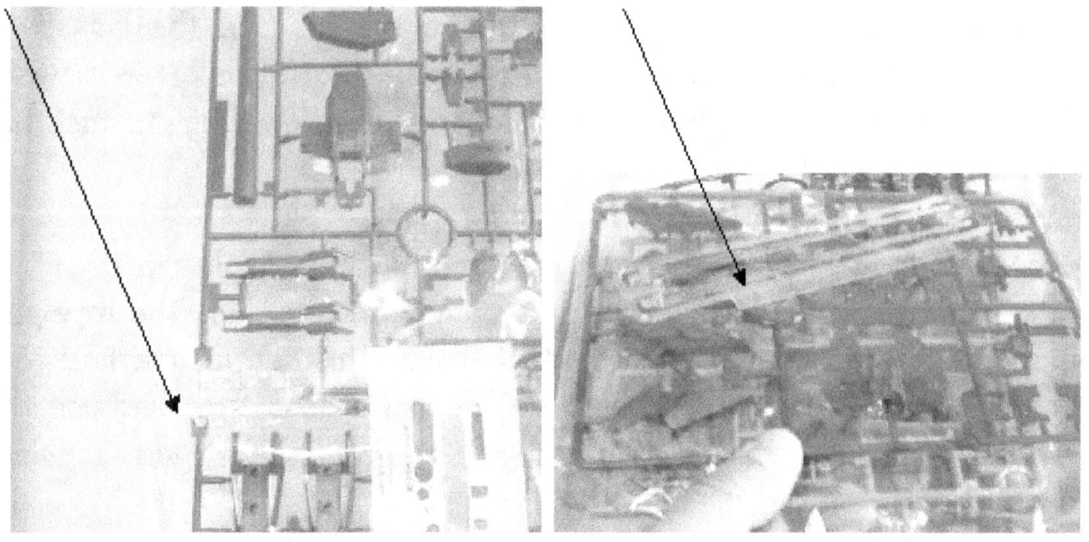

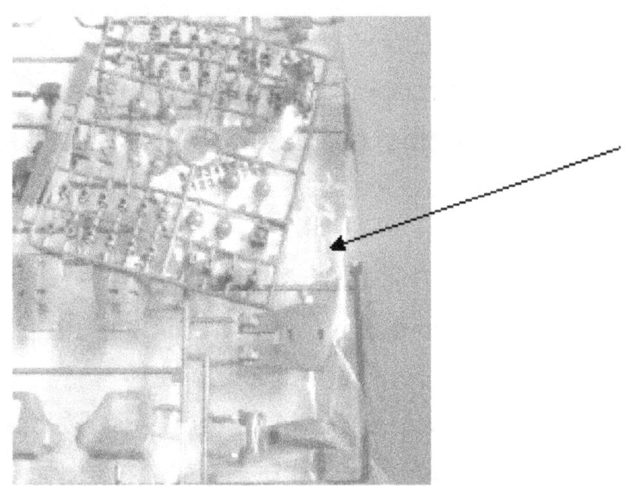

Clear parts are sometimes quite badly scratched due to poor packaging. Even though clear parts can be sanded for removing scratches and minor damages, for beginners it is simply too difficult. Remember, when a damage is made to the clear plastic, it will be very difficult to polish back the clarity. Therefore, don't do this on your first few Gundam models.

Sanding clear parts is possible, but it requires a very different approach than sanding regular plastic parts, and it comes with significant risks. The main problem is that sanding inevitably creates microscopic scratches in the clear plastic, and these scratches will scatter light rather than allowing it to pass through cleanly. The result is a cloudy, frosted, milky appearance instead of the crystal clear transparency you want for a window or canopy.

However, if you have a clear part with a visible seam line, a raised mold mark, or a rough edge that needs to be removed, you can sand it successfully if you follow a meticulous process. The key is to understand that sanding is only the first step, and you must fully restore the polish afterward.

If you absolutely must sand a clear part, you should start with a very fine grit sandpaper, never anything coarse. Begin around 600 or 800 grit and work progressively up through 1500, 2000, 3000, and finally 6000 grit or higher. The goal is to replace the large scratches from each grit with progressively finer scratches that become invisible to the naked eye. You must sand wet rather than dry, using water or a mild soapy solution as a lubricant. Wet sanding prevents the sandpaper from clogging, reduces heat buildup that could craze the plastic, and helps carry away the fine dust that would otherwise embed itself in the plastic surface.

After sanding through the finest grit, the part will still look hazy or translucent rather than transparent. This is where polishing comes in. You need to use a plastic polishing compound, such as those made by Novus, Tamiya, or Meguiar's for headlight restoration. Start with a coarse or medium polish and work your way to a fine or finishing polish. Apply the polish with a soft, lint-free cloth or a cotton swab, using circular motions and moderate pressure. For the final step, a liquid gloss coating like Future Floor Polish or an acrylic clear gloss can be dipped or brushed onto the part to fill any remaining micro-scratches and restore optical clarity.

Given the complexity and risk of this process, you should consider alternatives before sanding a clear part. If the part has a mold seam line running across it, you can often remove it by carefully scraping with the back of a hobby knife blade rather than sanding. Hold the blade perpendicular to the surface and draw it gently along the seam line to shave off the raised plastic. This leaves a much smoother surface that requires less polishing. Another alternative is to simply hide the seam line by positioning the part so the seam faces away from view or by framing it with painted details. Some modelers also choose to dip their clear parts in Future Floor Polish before any sanding or gluing, as the thick liquid can sometimes fill light scratches and seam lines well enough that sanding becomes unnecessary.

For small imperfections like dust specks or tiny bubbles in the clear plastic itself, you are often better off leaving them alone than attempting to sand and polish, because the risk of making the problem worse is very high. A tiny speck that is barely noticeable becomes a large cloudy patch after aggressive sanding.

The bottom line is that you can sand clear parts, but only if you are prepared to commit to the full progressive sanding and polishing process. If you do not have the patience or the proper materials to polish the part back to clarity, you should avoid sanding altogether. For most modelers, the safest approach is to use a sharp blade to scrape away any obvious mold lines and then dip the part in a clear gloss coating, which often yields excellent results without any sanding at all.

Polycaps and clamshells

Polycaps (short for polyurethane caps, also known as poly-caps or PVC caps) are small, soft, grey or black rubbery plastic connectors. Unlike the hard, brittle styrene plastic that makes up most of the model, polycaps are flexible and slightly spongy. Their purpose is to create moving joints. For example, in a car model, polycaps are often inserted into the wheel hubs. The axle pin on the suspension then snaps into the polycap, allowing the wheels to spin freely and stay firmly attached at the same time. In action figure or mecha kits, polycaps are used for shoulders, elbows, and knees so the joints can be posed repeatedly without becoming loose or wearing out. The key advantage is that polycaps grip metal or plastic axles tightly but still allow movement, whereas a hard plastic-on-plastic joint would either be too stiff to move or would grind itself loose over time. Because polycaps are made of a different material than the rest of the kit, you need to use a different adhesive. Standard plastic cement will not work on polycaps, as it only melts styrene plastic. You should use super glue or epoxy if you absolutely need to glue a polycap in place, but usually they are designed to be press-fitted and require no glue at all.

Clamshells refer to a specific way that certain model parts are molded. A clamshell part is one that comes in two halves, left and right or top and bottom, that join together to form a hollow finished shape. The classic example is an aircraft fuselage, which typically comes as a left half and a right half that you glue together along the center seam. Another example is a car body, which might be molded as a single piece with an opening clamshell-like hood or trunk, or a motorcycle fuel tank that comes in two halves that close around an internal frame. The term "clamshell" is also used to describe the assembly process itself, where you take the two halves and close them like, appropriately, a clam. The challenge with clamshell assemblies is that the seam line where the two halves meet almost always requires putty and sanding to hide completely. Additionally, you often need to install interior details, such as a cockpit, engine, or landing gear bay, before closing the clamshell because once the halves are glued together, you can no longer reach inside. For this reason, dry-fitting the clamshell halves before gluing is essential to make sure everything inside fits properly and the two halves come together without gaps.

Polycaps are extremely prevalent in Gunpla, particularly in High Grade and Master Grade kits. These soft, rubbery pieces usually come on their own dedicated runner labeled PC, and their main purpose is to create smooth, movable joints at the shoulders, elbows, hips, and knees, allowing your finished Gundam model to be posed and re-posed without the joints becoming loose too quickly. When you assemble a Gunpla, you will often find that you need to sandwich a polycap between two hard plastic parts. For example, a polycap fits into a socket in the upper arm, and a peg from the forearm plugs into it, creating a secure yet flexible elbow joint. This design is part of what makes Gunpla accessible to beginners, as it reduces the need for glue and allows for easy assembly. However, polycaps do have a downside. Over time and with repeated handling, the rubbery material can wear out and lose its grip strength, causing limbs to become floppy or unable to hold up heavy weapons. Because of this, Bandai has been moving away from polycaps in some newer kit designs, particularly in more recent Real Grade and Master Grade releases, opting instead for engineering that uses hard plastic-on-plastic joints for better long-term stability.

The clamshell concept is equally common in Gunpla, though it might not always be called by that name. In Gunpla, clamshell assemblies refer to parts that are made of two halves that close together around an internal structure. A perfect example is a Gundam's lower leg or forearm, which are typically molded as a front half and a back half. During assembly, you might place internal frame parts or polycaps inside one half, and then close the other half over the top.

High Grade kits are particularly known for using clamshell chassis parts. For instance, the torso section of an HG kit often uses clamshell pieces that close around internal polycaps to tie the whole upper body together. This technique allows for hollow parts that are lightweight but still detailed on the outside, and it simplifies the molding process. The challenge with clamshell parts in Gunpla is the same as with any model kit: the seam line where the two halves meet. These seams often run right down the middle of a prominently visible part, like the front of a shin or forearm, and may require sanding or putty work to remove if you want a pristine finish.

Using Surfacer

Surfacer is a specialized liquid primer that serves multiple essential purposes in plastic modeling, and it is one of those products that once you start using it, you wonder how you ever managed without it. Available in spray cans or bottles for airbrushing, with popular brands including Mr. Surfacer from Mr. Hobby and Tamiya's Liquid Surface Primer, surfacer is thicker and more filling than standard primer paint.

The primary purpose of surfacer is to reveal and fix surface imperfections before you apply your final color coats. When you have finished sanding seams, filling gaps with putty, and generally preparing your model, the plastic surface may look perfectly smooth to your naked eye. However, once you spray on a coat of surfacer, it dries to a uniform matte finish that acts like a truth serum for the surface. Every tiny scratch, pinhole, low spot, or uneven seam that you missed will suddenly become visible because the surfacer settles differently into these imperfections. This allows you to see exactly where you need to do more sanding or apply a little more putty before committing to your final paint job. In this way, surfacer saves you from the heartbreaking moment of seeing all your hidden flaws appear only after you have applied your expensive color coats.

The second major purpose of surfacer is to fill very fine scratches and minor imperfections automatically. Surfacer contains microscopic particles that settle into scratches as fine as 600 to 1000 grit sandpaper marks. When you spray a light coat over a properly sanded surface, the surfacer fills these micro-scratches and creates a perfectly smooth, uniform base for your paint. This is particularly important for achieving glossy finishes on car models or any kit where you want a mirror-like shine, because any remaining scratch will ruin the final gloss. Different grades of surfacer are available for this purpose, with Mr. Surfacer 500 being quite thick for filling larger scratches and minor pinholes, Mr. Surfacer 1000 being a good all-purpose middle grade, and Mr. Surfacer 1200 and 1500 being very fine for final surface preparation before gloss coats.

The third purpose of surfacer is to provide a uniform color base underneath your paint. Plastic model kits often come in multiple colors of styrene, such as gray, white, tan, and even red or blue on the same runner. If you painted a light color like yellow or white directly over these different colored plastics, the final shade would appear uneven because the plastic color would show through. Surfacer, typically being light gray or white, creates a consistent neutral base so that your color coats look exactly as intended regardless of what color plastic is underneath. Additionally, surfacer contains etching agents that bite slightly into the plastic, giving your subsequent paint layers something to grip onto. This dramatically improves paint adhesion and makes your final finish much more resistant to chipping or peeling when you handle the model or apply masking tape.

Some surfacers also come in different colors for specific applications. White surfacer is excellent for preparing models that will be painted bright colors like white, yellow, or red, as it provides a bright base that makes these colors pop. Black surfacer is used as a base for metallic paints like silver or chrome, as a glossy black undercoat creates a deep, reflective shine. For most general modeling work, a light gray surfacer is the best all-purpose choice.

To use surfacer, you simply spray it over your assembled and sanded model in light, even coats. After it dries, which usually takes about fifteen to thirty minutes, you can inspect the surface. If you see any remaining imperfections, you sand those areas lightly with fine grit sandpaper, apply more putty if needed, and then spray another coat of surfacer. Once you are satisfied that the surface is perfect, you can proceed directly to your primer and then your color coats, or in many cases, thinned surfacer can act as both primer and surface preparer in one step.

The Mr. Surfacer from Mr. Hobby can be used for filling in bumps, dents, scratches, as well as for removing bubbles and finishing bases. Simply put, it can be used as sort of a soluble putty. The general recommendation made by vendor is to use Surfacer 500 for general surface work and use dissolved putty for evening up the surface rough sections.

8506

MR.SURFACER 1000 SPRAY

| Detail

Mr.SURFACER 1000 contains finer granules than M the same way but ,due to the finer granules after s corrected surface is possible. Available in bottle ar

The number indicates coarseness. The larger the number the finer the granules after sanding.

Using Gundam Markers

Gundam Markers are alcohol-based paint pens designed specifically for customizing Gunpla, or Gundam plastic models. They offer a simple and affordable way to add detail, apply color, and achieve professional-looking results without needing an airbrush or traditional paints. There are several types of Gundam Markers, each made for a different task such as panel lining, painting small details, or applying metallic finishes.

The most common types include fine-tip markers, pour-type markers, brush-type markers, Real Touch markers, and eraser markers. Fine-tip markers have a hard plastic tip and are used like a pen for basic panel lining, which means drawing into the recessed grooves of the model to add shadow and definition. They are a good choice for beginners and come in colors such as black, gray, and brown. Pour-type markers also have a hard plastic tip, but instead of drawing with them, you simply touch the tip to a panel line and the ink flows automatically by capillary action, filling the groove instantly and much faster than tracing. Brush-type markers have a soft, brush-like tip and are used for painting larger areas, adding details, or applying metallic finishes like gold or silver. Real Touch markers are water-based and have dual fine and broad tips, making them ideal for shading, weathering, and creating grime effects because the ink is easy to blend and erase. Finally, the eraser marker contains a special solution that removes dried marker ink from plastic without damaging the surface, making it very useful for cleaning up mistakes.

Using Gundam Markers correctly involves a few key steps regardless of which type you are using. First, you should always shake the marker vigorously with the cap on to mix the internal ink and the mixing ball inside, and this is especially vital for metallic markers. Next, you need to prime the tip by pressing it down on a piece of scrap paper or a plastic palette until the ink flows consistently, being careful not to push too hard or the ink may drip out. For panel lining with a fine-tip marker, you simply trace the tip along the recessed lines of the plastic, letting the tip sit in the groove so surface tension helps guide the ink. For a pour-type marker, you should never draw with it; instead, just touch the tip to a panel line and watch the ink wick through the groove on its own. For brush-type markers, which act like small paintbrushes, you shake them well and then apply the ink directly to plastic surfaces. For very small details, you can press the marker tip to let a drop of paint pool out and then use a separate fine brush to apply that drop with precision. Metallic markers are excellent for creating shiny accents on parts like sword blades, thrusters, or inner frames, and applying them with gentle, even pressure gives the best finish.

Cleanup is straightforward and mistakes are easy to fix. If you make a mistake while panel lining, you can often wipe away the wet ink immediately with your fingertip or a tissue. For dried ink, the eraser marker is very effective because you apply it over the mistake, let it sit for a moment, and then wipe it away. You can also use a cotton swab lightly dipped in isopropyl alcohol or lighter fluid to clean up smudges and overflow from fine-tip and pour-type markers.

There are some important warnings to keep in mind. For the most natural panel lining look, you should use gray ink on white or light colored parts, black ink on dark or blue parts, and brown ink on red or yellow parts. While the ink may feel dry to the touch in just a few minutes, it actually takes at least twenty-four hours to fully cure, so you should allow for proper drying time before heavy handling. The most critical warning is that the solvents in standard Gundam Markers can damage ABS plastic, causing it to become brittle and crack. Most Gunpla inner frames are made of ABS, so you should check your kit's manual and avoid applying marker directly to ABS runners. Additionally, you should avoid using standard fine-tip or pour-type markers over painted surfaces, because the solvent will melt the paint film, ruining your work and clogging the marker tip. If you need to panel line over painted surfaces, you should use water-based options or apply a clear top coat before panel lining. In summary, Gundam Markers are a fantastic tool for detailing Gunpla, but they require some care regarding plastic types and drying times to achieve the best results.

Mr. Hobby is best known for offering "package" of markers (in the form of SIX PACK) for specific Gundam models.

The SIX PACK offerings are model-specific.

The markers are available in different sizes and brush shapes.

This eraser is for removing the marker paint.

The variations include metallic, flourescent and basic colors. Most of them use alcohol based inks.

You can absolutely paint an entire model using only Gundam Markers and nothing else, but there are important limitations and trade-offs to understand before committing to this approach. Many builders have successfully completed entire kits using only markers, particularly smaller scales like High Grade or SD kits, but the results and the process will differ significantly from using an airbrush or spray cans. The main advantage of using only markers is convenience. However, there are several practical challenges to painting an entire kit with markers. The first is coverage. Gundam Markers apply a relatively thin layer of ink compared to airbrushed or spray can paint. On large, flat surfaces such as a Gundam's shoulder armor, chest plate, or shield, you will likely see brush strokes no matter how carefully you apply the ink, especially with lighter colors. Achieving an even, streak-free finish on a large area requires multiple thin coats and a great deal of patience, with adequate drying time between each coat. Even then, the final result may still show some unevenness when viewed up close.

The second challenge is color consistency. Gundam Markers come in a limited range of colors compared to the vast selection available in bottled paints. You can certainly find the classic Gundam colors such as white, red, blue, yellow, and gray, along with some metallic and specialty shades. But if you want a specific custom shade, like a particular olive green or a muted mauve, you cannot mix marker inks together the way you can mix liquid paints. You are restricted to whatever colors Bandai offers in marker form.

The third challenge is consumption and cost. Painting an entire model kit with markers consumes a surprising amount of ink. A single marker may not be enough to cover a whole Master Grade kit, especially if you are painting over dark plastic with a light color. You might need two or even three markers of the same color to complete one model, and at several dollars per marker, the cost can quickly exceed that of a small bottle of paint and a brush. Additionally, the marker tips can become frayed or worn down over the course of painting a large model, making application increasingly difficult.

The fourth challenge is working around the limitations of the marker tip itself. The brush-type markers have reasonably wide tips, but they are still much smaller than a typical paintbrush used for large surfaces. Painting a big area like a Gundam's leg or wing becomes a slow, tedious process of laying down many parallel strokes and trying to blend them together before the ink dries. Getting into tight corners or recessed details is easy, but achieving a smooth finish on broad, open areas is genuinely difficult.

There is also the issue of durability. Marker ink is alcohol-based and bonds reasonably well to bare plastic, but it is not as tough as properly primed and topcoated airbrush paint. The marker finish can be scratched or rubbed off with handling, especially on high-friction areas like joints or edges that your fingers touch frequently. If you want your marker-only paint job to last, you really should apply a clear top coat over the entire model, which means introducing at least one additional product beyond the markers themselves.

That said, many builders have had great success with marker-only painting by choosing their kits wisely and adjusting their expectations. Small kits with smaller surface areas, such as SD or Entry Grade Gundams, are much more manageable than large Master Grade or Perfect Grade kits. Kits with naturally broken-up surface detail, where large flat areas are broken by panel lines, vents, or color separation, hide brush strokes much better than smooth, minimalist designs. Darker colors also tend to look more forgiving than light colors like white or yellow, which show every imperfection. Some builders embrace the slightly hand-painted, textured look as a stylistic choice rather than a flaw, giving their model a unique character that differs from the flawless factory finish of an airbrushed kit. If you decide to try painting an entire kit with only markers anyway, there are techniques that will improve your results. Shaking the markers very thoroughly before every use ensures the ink is fully mixed. Applying multiple thin coats rather than one thick coat prevents puddling and reduces visible strokes. Allowing each coat to dry completely, which can take thirty minutes or more depending on humidity, prevents the new ink from reactivating and lifting the layer beneath. Working in a consistent direction for each section, such as always stroking from top to bottom, helps minimize the appearance of brush marks. Finally, spraying a clear flat or gloss top coat from a can over the finished marker work will protect the ink and unify the sheen across the entire model.

Applying panel lining with markers

Applying panel lines with Gundam Markers is one of the most satisfying and transformative techniques you can learn as a builder, as it adds depth and definition to your model with relatively little effort. The process differs slightly depending on whether you are using a fine-tip marker or a pour-type marker, but the overall goal is the same: getting dark ink into the recessed lines of the plastic while keeping it off the raised surfaces.

Before you begin, you should make sure your model is fully assembled at least to the point where the parts whose panel lines you want to line are in place. Some builders prefer to panel line while the parts are still on the runner, while others do it after assembly. Working on the runner can be easier for holding small parts, but panel lines that cross seam lines or joints will be interrupted. Working after assembly gives you a complete picture but requires more careful handling. Either way, you should start with clean plastic free of dust, oils from your fingers, or mold release agents, so wiping the model down with a mild soap and water or a quick wipe with isopropyl alcohol before you begin is a good habit.

If you are using a fine-tip marker, the process is very straightforward. You shake the marker well with the cap on, then press the tip down on a piece of scrap paper until the ink begins to flow. Once the tip is primed, you simply draw the marker along each recessed panel line, letting the tip ride in the groove. You do not need to press hard; the ink will flow from the tip into the line with very light pressure. For long, continuous lines, try to make one steady stroke from beginning to end rather than multiple short strokes, because stopping and starting can leave uneven deposits of ink. When you reach the end of a line, lift the marker cleanly. If you accidentally go outside the line or make a wobbly mark, do not panic. The ink takes a few seconds to dry, so you can often wipe away a mistake immediately with your fingertip or a tissue. For ink that has already dried, you can use a cotton swab lightly dampened with isopropyl alcohol or lighter fluid to clean it up.

If you are using a pour-type marker, also known as a flow-type or panel lining marker, the method is completely different and actually faster. After shaking the marker and priming the tip, you do not draw with it at all. Instead, you simply touch the tip to a panel line at any point along its length, and the ink will automatically wick or flow through the entire groove by capillary action. It is almost like magic to watch. The ink travels along the line in both directions from the point of contact, filling the recess completely without any effort on your part. You then move to the next line, touch the tip again, and repeat. The pour-type marker leaves a cleaner, more consistent line than the fine-tip version, and it is much faster for kits with many long panel lines. The downside is that the ink is thinner and more prone to spreading, so cleanup is almost always required. The pour-type marker almost always leaves small dots or smudges at the point where you touched the tip, as well as occasional overflow where the ink escapes the line. You simply let the ink dry for a few minutes, then take a cotton swab lightly dampened with isopropyl alcohol or lighter fluid and gently wipe across the line, perpendicular to its direction. This removes the excess ink from the raised surfaces while leaving the ink safely inside the recessed line. Some builders prefer to use lighter fluid because it evaporates faster and is less likely to damage the plastic, but isopropyl alcohol works perfectly well as long as you do not soak the plastic.

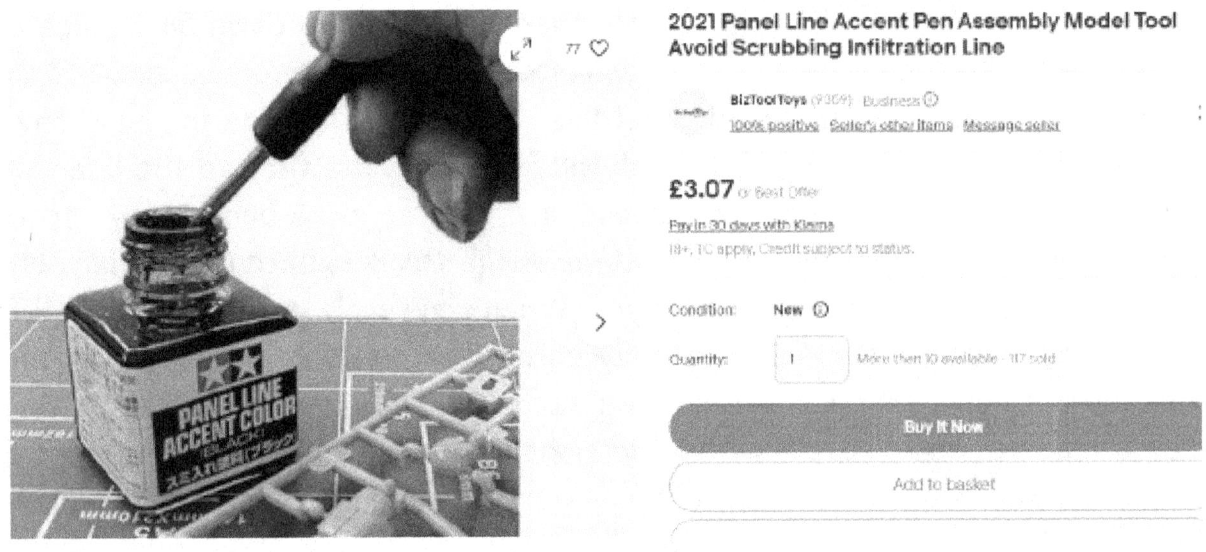

Regardless of which type of marker you use, there are some universal tips that will improve your results. Always let the panel lining ink dry completely before you attempt any cleanup. If you try to wipe away excess ink while it is still wet, you will often just smear it around and make a bigger mess. Waiting ten to fifteen minutes allows the ink to set so that it resists being pulled out of the panel line when you wipe across it. Use a cotton swab that is damp but not dripping wet, because too much liquid can seep into the panel line and dissolve the ink you want to keep. Roll the cotton swab as you wipe rather than dragging it in one direction, which helps lift the ink off the surface rather than pushing it around. For very tight areas or corners, you can flatten the tip of a wooden cocktail stick and wrap a tiny piece of tissue or cloth around it to create a precision cleaning tool.

Choosing the right color marker for your plastic is also important for achieving a natural look. On white or very light gray plastic, you should use gray panel lining ink. Black on white can look too harsh and cartoonish, though some builders prefer that high-contrast anime look. On blue, dark gray, or black plastic, you should use black ink. On red, yellow, or orange plastic, brown ink gives a much warmer and more natural shadow than black. Many builders keep all three colors on hand and switch between them depending on the part.

If you plan to apply a top coat over your model after panel lining, you should be aware that the solvents in some spray top coats can reactivate alcohol-based marker ink and cause it to bleed or run. To prevent this, you should either use a water-based clear coat, apply your top coat in very light mist coats that dry almost instantly, or simply wait a full twenty-four hours for the marker ink to cure completely before top coating. Even then, testing on a scrap piece first is always wise.

There are panel markers of different sizes. HGs and RGs usually have smaller panel lines while MGs have bigger lines.

Using primer

With a primer applied prior to actual painting, the paint can stick onto the plastic surface much easier. Technically speaking, priming is a process that seals the surface for ensuring better adhesion of paint to the model and increasing paint durability.

Do note that some primers can dissolve plastic surface. They may also not work well with the kind of paint you use. Therefore, TEST them out before use.

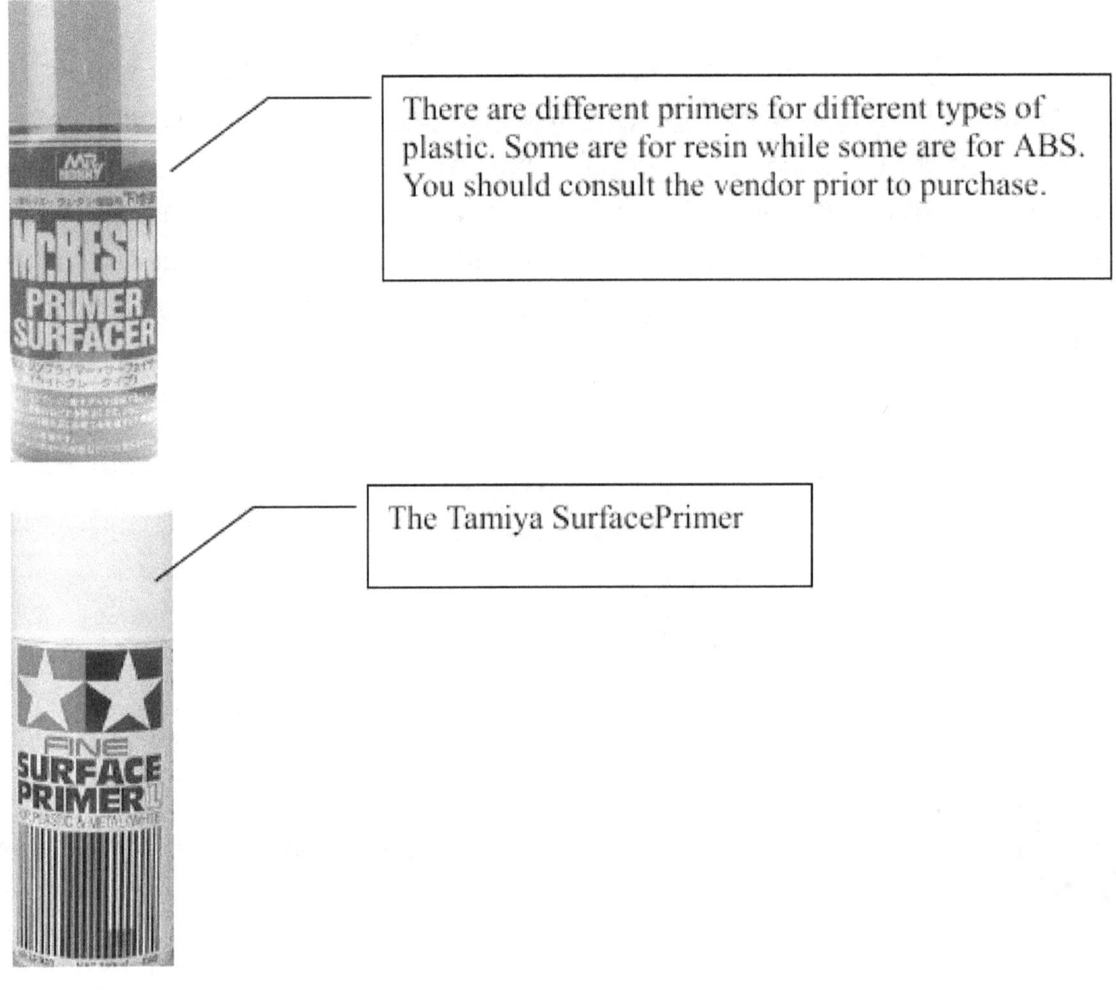

There are different primers for different types of plastic. Some are for resin while some are for ABS. You should consult the vendor prior to purchase.

The Tamiya SurfacePrimer

Applying decals

Do this after the painting process is completely done (and that the paint is totally dried). Most kits come with a sticker guide for you to follow.

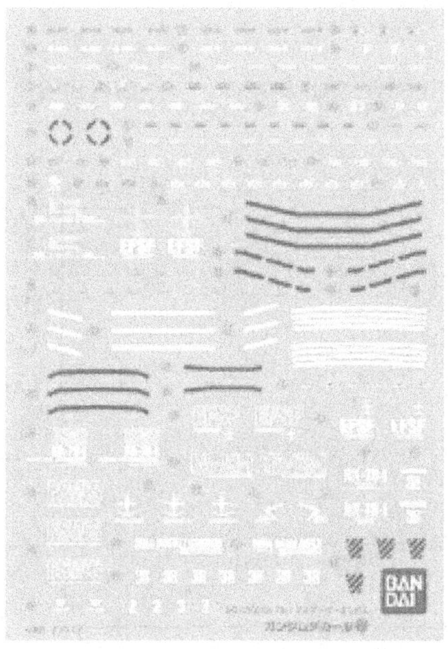

Typically you cut out the desired sticker from the sticker sheet, then soak it in water for a few seconds and then slide it right onto the plastic surface. Use a small piece of paper towel to pat dry the surface.

Along the process you should press on the sticker with a cotton swab to get rid of air bubbles.

Stickers are very difficult (if not impossible) to move once they are in place. Therefore, plan the sticker placement and think twice before actual application.

You soften the stickers so they can adhere to curved surfaces (ie the decal needs to form a shape) much easier. To make the stickers softer you may use the Mr. Mark Softer. Keep in mind, as soon as you apply the sticker will get soft almost immediately, Therefore the decal must be in the right position when you are ready to go.

Mark Setter serves a different purpose – it ensures the decal sticker can truly stick to the surface.

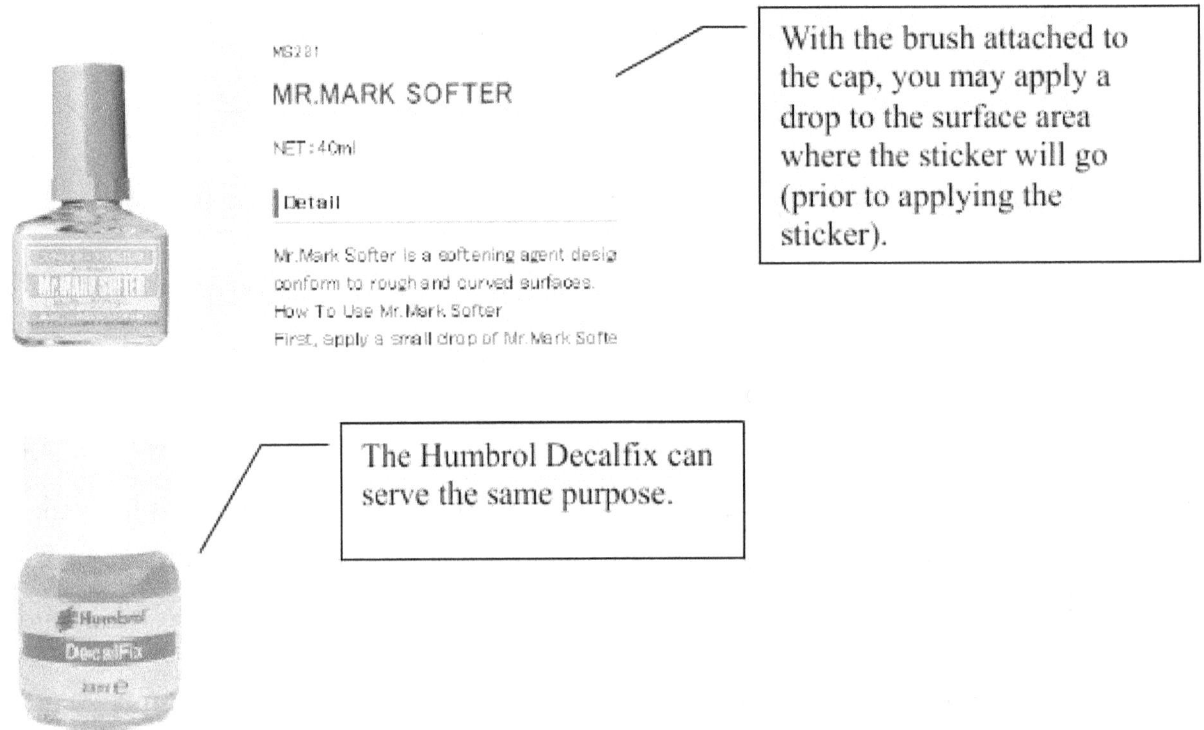

With the brush attached to the cap, you may apply a drop to the surface area where the sticker will go (prior to applying the sticker).

The Humbrol Decalfix can serve the same purpose.

After drying, prick the sticker with a needle to release the air. Then give a tiny drop of Mr. Mark Setter through the needled hole and apply pressure onto the sticker accordingly.

 HobbyPRESS.net (Hong Kong).

Mr. Mark Setter gives greater adhesiveness to the stickers.

There are replacement stickers widely available for the more popular Gundam models so you shouldn't need to worry about breaking any of those.

Choosing a model paint

Choosing paint for your Gunpla comes down to three main types of paint, and your decision will depend on your priorities such as ease of use, durability, or the ability to use specialized techniques. For a beginner, water-based acrylics are almost always the best place to start because they are low-odor, clean up with water or alcohol, and are very forgiving. However, understanding the full spectrum of hobby paints, including lacquers and enamels, is worth your time because the distinctions between them are what allow advanced builders to achieve professional results.

Water-based acrylics, such as those from Vallejo, Citadel, or Mr. Hobby Aqueous, are the most beginner-friendly option. They have low toxicity and very little odor, making them safe to use indoors without a heavy-duty spray booth, and you can clean your brushes with simple tap water or isopropyl alcohol. The trade-off is that standard water-based acrylics are generally less durable than lacquers. They can be prone to scratching if you handle the model frequently, so applying a clear top coat is highly recommended to protect your work. On the opposite end of the spectrum are lacquer-based paints, which include Mr. Color from GSI Creos, Gaia Notes, and many of the Gundam Color spray cans. Lacquers are beloved by experienced builders because they dry incredibly fast, dry rock-hard, and are very resistant to scratches. They also level out beautifully when airbrushed, leaving almost no visible brush strokes. However, the fumes from lacquer thinner are very strong and toxic, requiring a proper spray booth or excellent ventilation and a respirator. They are also more complex to clean up, requiring specific chemical thinners rather than water.

The third category is enamel paints, most commonly represented by Tamiya's square jars. Builders rarely paint an entire model with enamels because they take a very long time to dry, sometimes eight hours or more, which can trap dust in the finish. However, enamels are the gold standard for one specific task: panel lining. Because enamel thinner is hotter than acrylics but gentler than lacquers, you can apply an enamel wash over a fully cured lacquer or acrylic paint job. When you wipe away the excess with a cotton swab dampened with enamel thinner or even lighter fluid, the thinner removes the enamel from the raised surfaces without damaging the paint layers underneath. But you must be very careful, as enamel thinner pooled in joints can make ABS plastic brittle and crack, so always test on the runner first.

To summarize the characteristics of each type, water-based acrylics are very easy to use, dry in about thirty minutes, have moderate durability that typically requires a top coat, have low odor and toxicity, and are suitable for full painting and base coats. Lacquers are for more advanced users, dry in ten to fifteen minutes, have very high scratch-resistant durability, have high odor and toxicity requiring a respirator, and are excellent for both full painting and top coats. Enamels are intermediate in difficulty, take six to eight hours or more to dry, have low durability for handling, have moderate odor, and are primarily used for panel lining and weathering rather than painting entire models.

When it comes to recommended brands to get you started, sticking with known hobby names will save you a lot of frustration because general craft store paints have large pigment particles that will obscure the fine surface details of your Gunpla. For water-based acrylics, Vallejo Mecha Color is designed specifically for articulated models like Gunpla and has excellent resistance to scratching from posing. Mr. Hobby Aqueous is a water-based lacquer that behaves like an acrylic but has hardness closer to a lacquer, making it an excellent middle-ground choice.

For lacquers, Mr. Color and Gaia Notes are the industry standards for high-end finishes. GPaint offers a very user-friendly, pre-thinned lacquer that boasts being primerless and baseless, meaning you do not need a black undercoat for metallics, which is great for saving time. For convenience, Gundam Markers are an entire ecosystem of paint, with most standard markers being lacquer-based, the pour-type panel liners being enamel-based, and the Real Touch markers being oil-based. They are perfect for small details or touch-ups, but painting an entire kit with markers can be expensive and may leave visible stroke marks on large, flat surfaces.

If you are painting your very first Gundam, a hybrid approach that utilizes the strengths of each paint type while keeping the process safe and manageable is highly recommended. First, prime the model using a spray can of Mr. Surfacer, which is a lacquer, working outdoors or in a well-ventilated area to give your paint something to bite into. Second, paint the main colors using water-based acrylics like Vallejo or Aqueous by hand brush or spray can. Third, apply your decals, whether stickers or waterslides. Fourth, spray a clear gloss top coat using a spray can to seal the acrylic paint and create a smooth surface for the next step. Fifth, apply panel lines using the pour-type Gundam Marker, which is enamel-based, or Tamiya Panel Line Accent Color. Sixth, clean up the excess panel liner using a cotton swab lightly dipped in lighter fluid. Finally, finish with a final top coat, with flat or matte being popular for Gundams, to seal everything and give the model a uniform, non-toy-like appearance. This approach limits your exposure to strong chemicals by only using lacquer for the initial primer and final top coat, and it ensures that if you make a mistake with the enamel panel liner, you can wipe it off without damaging the acrylic paint underneath.

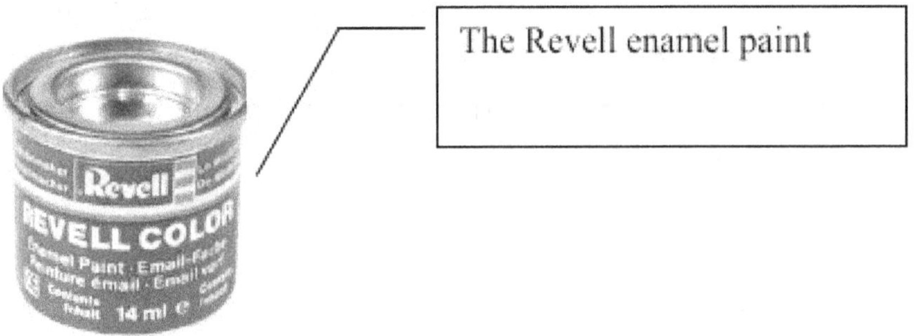

The Revell enamel paint

Acrylic paint is fast drying. It contains pigment suspension in acrylic polymer emulsion. In theory, acrylic paints can be diluted with water (the Humbrol acrylic paints are water based). The fast evaporation of water from the acrylic paint makes drying relatively fast. Do note that the paint will actually become water-resistant once dried. In practice, vendors often recommend that you use acrylic thinner.

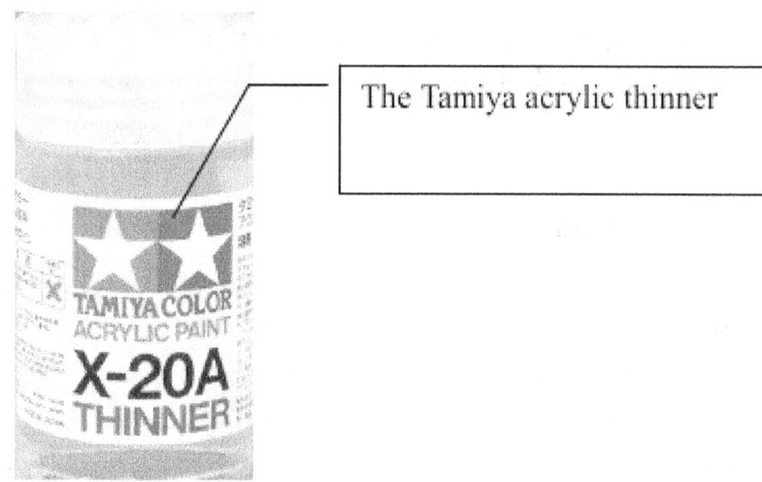

Laquer paint is a very "strong" paint. You need laquer thinner to work with it. Once dried it is not easily scratched.

Different people have different preferences. You may want to try them out and make your very own choice.

Do note that different paints react differently to different thinners. Some say 1:1 is best while some prefer 0.5:1.

My suggestion is that you should test out the mix on something else first. It may be a good idea to test paint the mix on the runner frame and see how it goes.

You determine the proportion that works best for you through experiment.

Pouring thinner directly into the original paint bottle is usually not recommended because it changes the entire bottle of paint permanently, making it unsuitable for other applications such as hand brushing, and it can also cause the paint to degrade over time if the ratio is incorrect or if the thinner reacts with the paint formula in ways that are not reversible.

The better and more common practice is to transfer a small amount of paint out of the original bottle into a separate container and then thin that portion. You can use a cheap plastic palette, a small disposable cup, a metal mixing tray, or even the bottom of a soda can. This approach allows you to experiment with different thinning ratios for different tasks without ruining your entire bottle of paint. For example, paint that is thinned for airbrushing, which typically requires a milk-like consistency, is usually too thin for hand brushing, where you want a slightly thicker consistency that will not run into panel lines or pool in corners. By thinning only what you need, you keep the rest of the bottle at its original factory consistency, ready for future use in any application.

There are, however, a few exceptions where pouring thinner directly into the bottle is acceptable or even intended. Some paint brands, such as Mr. Color and Tamiya, produce their paints quite thick specifically so that the user can thin them to their preferred consistency. Many experienced modelers do pour thinner into these bottles, but they do so carefully and with experience, knowing exactly how much thinner to add. Even then, they typically add thinner incrementally, shaking thoroughly between additions, and they rarely add enough to reach the final airbrushing consistency all at once. Instead, they might add just enough to make the paint flow better for hand brushing, and then for airbrushing they still transfer paint out and thin it further. Some newer paints, such as GPaint and certain pre-thinned lacquers, are sold ready to spray and should never have thinner added directly to the bottle because they are already at the optimal consistency.

If you decide to thin paint in a separate container, the process is straightforward. You pour or scoop a small amount of paint into your mixing container, approximately the size of a grape or a small coin depending on how much you need. Then you add thinner drop by drop, starting with roughly one drop of thinner for every two or three drops of paint. Stir or mix thoroughly with an old brush or a cocktail stick, then test the consistency. For hand brushing, you want the paint to flow smoothly off the brush without being so runny that it behaves like water. For airbrushing, you want it to have the consistency of skim milk, meaning it coats the side of the container and flows back down leaving a thin, translucent film. You can always add more thinner, but you cannot remove it, so go slowly.

The type of thinner you use is just as important as how you use it. You should always use the thinner that is designed for your specific brand and type of paint whenever possible. Tamiya X-20A is for Tamiya acrylics, Mr. Color Thinner is for Mr. Color lacquers, Vallejo Airbrush Thinner is for Vallejo water-based acrylics, and so on. Using the wrong thinner, such as using lacquer thinner in water-based acrylics, can cause the paint to curdle, clump, or become unusable. That said, some thinners are versatile. Isopropyl alcohol works well with many water-based acrylics and with Tamiya acrylics, and hardware store lacquer thinner can work with hobby lacquers, but it is harsher and may damage plastic if used carelessly. Lighter fluid is excellent for thinning enamel panel liners but should not be used to thin paint for painting large surfaces.

For a beginner, the safest and most practical method is to keep a few empty dropper bottles or small glass jars on hand. You can buy empty squeeze bottles with fine tips, often called "eye dropper bottles" or "paint mixing bottles," for very little money. You pour your paint into one of these, add your thinner drop by drop using a pipette or the dropper tip of your thinner bottle, close the lid, and shake vigorously. This creates a custom-thinned batch of paint that you can store for later without altering your original bottle. Label the bottle with the paint color and the ratio of paint to thinner you used so you can replicate it in the future.

Just like most chemicals, model paints do have a limited life span. Proper packaging can increase the shelf life a bit though.

Mixing paints

You should not mix acrylic paint with enamel paint to produce a custom color. The reason is that acrylic paints are water-based or alcohol-based, while enamel paints are oil-based. They are chemically incompatible and will not truly mix together. Instead of forming a smooth, uniform custom color, the two paints will separate, curdle, or form a clumpy, unusable mess. The pigments may clump together while the different binders repel each other, leaving you with a grainy, lumpy mixture that will not adhere properly to your model and will certainly not spray or brush smoothly. If you need a custom color, you should mix within the same paint family, such as mixing two different acrylics together or two different enamels together. For example, you can mix Tamiya acrylics with other Tamiya acrylics or with Mr. Hobby Aqueous, and you can mix Testors enamels with other Testors enamels. Never mix across families.

In contrast, using different paints on different coats is actually a very common and powerful technique in advanced modeling. You absolutely can apply different types of paint for different layers, and doing so strategically allows you to achieve effects that would be impossible with a single paint type. The key is to understand the order in which you apply them, based on the strength or "hotness" of the paint's solvent. The general rule is that you should apply hotter or stronger paints first, and then apply milder paints on top. Lacquers are the hottest, meaning they contain the strongest solvents. Enamels are intermediate. Water-based acrylics are the mildest, containing the weakest solvents. Therefore, a typical and very effective layering strategy is to start with a lacquer primer, then apply lacquer base colors, then apply enamel panel liners or washes, and finally apply water-based acrylics for small details or touch-ups. The reason this works is that once a lacquer layer has fully cured, it is very hard and resistant to mild solvents. When you apply an enamel wash over a cured lacquer finish, the enamel thinner will not damage the lacquer underneath. Similarly, when you apply a water-based acrylic detail over a cured enamel or lacquer layer, the water or alcohol in the acrylic will not harm the layers beneath.

The opposite order, applying mild paints first and hot paints on top, is where you will run into disaster. If you apply a water-based acrylic as your base coat and then spray a lacquer clear coat over it, the hot solvents in the lacquer will reactivate and dissolve the acrylic underneath, causing it to wrinkle, bubble, or lift entirely. In the same way, applying an enamel panel liner over an uncured or unprotected acrylic base coat can result in the enamel thinner eating through the acrylic and ruining your paint job. This is why experienced builders often seal their acrylic paint with a clear lacquer or enamel gloss coat before applying enamel washes, creating a barrier that protects the underlying paint.

The critical factor that makes all of this possible is allowing each layer to fully cure before applying the next. Drying time, where the paint feels dry to the touch, is not the same as curing time, where the paint has fully hardened and the solvents have completely evaporated. For water-based acrylics, curing can take twenty-four hours. For enamels, it can take forty-eight hours or more. For lacquers, curing is much faster, often just a few hours. If you rush and apply a hotter paint over a milder paint that is not fully cured, the milder paint may still contain residual solvents that will react unpredictably. Patience is the secret ingredient to successful multi-paint layering.

In case you need to mix colors, you need nothing other than thinner and an empty container to go ahead with the mixing process. Glass based container such as the Tamiya mixing jar recommended. There are several different sizes available. Plastic based container may not work well when solvent based paint is involved.

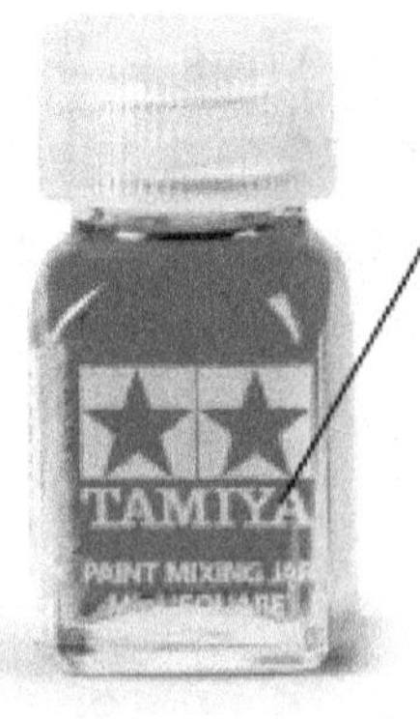

Spray painting

You can absolutely use Tamiya and Testors spray can paints on Gundam models, as both are widely used in the modeling community and can produce excellent results when applied correctly. Tamiya spray paints are generally the more popular choice among Gunpla builders, as their TS series designed for plastics works very well on Gundam models, and many builders have successfully used them for full repaints. Experienced modellers report that Tamiya sprays perform consistently and produce great finishes, particularly their clear coats which are highly regarded, and you will commonly find Tamiya sprays used for everything from base colors to topcoats in Gunpla projects. Testors spray paints are also a viable option, though there are some important considerations. Testors offers both enamel and acrylic formulations in spray cans, with the enamel-based sprays requiring longer drying times of typically twenty-four to forty-eight hours for a full cure, while acrylic versions dry in about thirty minutes to an hour. Both types can be used successfully, but they require proper surface preparation and application technique to achieve good results.

Priming is highly recommended regardless of which brand you choose. If the paint you use is very strong, then you can paint directly on the plastic surface without priming assuming you have rinsed the parts thoroughly. In any case you do NOT need more than two layers of primer.

Clear coats are also very important for protection and finish. Many builders seal their paint work with a clear top coat such as Testors Dullcote or Tamiya TS-80 Flat Clear, which protects the paint from handling and gives the model a uniform sheen. In any case, the primary purpose of top coat is protection – you want to protect your painted surface from scratches and other external threats. You do not need more than TWO top coats. I prefer to use Mr. Hobby's Mr. Top Coat in spray can form.

It is worth noting that while Testors Dullcote is a classic product, it has been discontinued in some regions, and Tamiya's clear coats are now a common and excellent alternative. You should be patient between layers and allow each coat of paint to dry thoroughly before applying the next. For enamel sprays, this is particularly important due to their longer curing time, as rushing can lead to undesirable reactions or a soft finish that is easily damaged.

There are several variations of the Mr. Top Coat line, giving different looks to the existing color surface (top coat, gloss, semi gloss, flat …etc).

Keep in mind, all these paints are made of chemical. None of them smells good. To be precise, almost all spray paints contain Volatile Organic Compounds VOCs that are emitted as gases. The most common VOCs that may be harmful include Acetone, Xylene and Toluene. Short-term side effects may include eye, nose and throat irritation as well as headaches, loss of coordination, and nausea. Long-term side effects can lead to problems with your liver, kidneys, and even the central nervous system.

To stay healthy you need proper ventilation. You should use spray paint in a paint booth, spray tent, or portable spray booth to better ventilate! If you have a deep pocket, consider to invest in a Mr. Super Booth. Or you can DIY an extractor fan. There are many DIY tutorials on youtube.

You can spray outdoor if wind is totally absent. A tiny bit of wind can disrupt your entire spraying effort. Also check your local regulations. You do not want to receive complaints from your neighbors.

You may use paint striper such as Modelstrip for removing paint without making damage to the model surface. All you need to do is to plaster the model all over with the paste in the concerned areas, then place the model in a plastic bag overnight (do make sure the bag is air tight). Wash the model with water and the paste will get washed off together with the unwanted paint.

Good quality brushes last longer even when stronger chemical is involved. However, those brushes for paper artwork painting should also work great as long as you take care of them properly after use. Generally, when applying acrylic paints you should use a taklon, kanekalon, or sable brush. When applying enamel/model paints you should use a stiff-bristle brush.

Clean them with the right kind of thinner after use. Specialized cleaner such as the Mr. Brush Washer will also do the trick.

The number of coats

When painting a model, the number of coats you apply depends on several factors including the type of paint you are using, the color you are applying, the color of the plastic underneath, and the finish you are trying to achieve.

However, a good general rule is that you should plan for two to three thin coats of paint, rather than one thick coat. This approach nearly always produces better results because thin coats dry faster, level more smoothly, and are much less likely to hide surface details or run into panel lines.

For a standard paint job using spray cans or an airbrush, you would typically start with a primer coat. One thin, even coat of primer is usually sufficient, though some builders prefer two very light primer coats to ensure full coverage. The primer does not need to be opaque; it just needs to provide a uniform surface for the color coats to grip. Once the primer is dry, you move to your base color. The first thin coat of color will often look patchy and translucent, especially if you are painting a light color like white or yellow over a dark primer or over bare plastic. This is normal and expected.

Do not be tempted to spray a heavy second coat to fix it immediately. Instead, let that first coat dry for the recommended time, which might be as little as ten minutes for lacquers or up to an hour for water-based acrylics, and then apply your second thin coat. The second coat will cover significantly more of the surface. For most colors on most surfaces, two thin coats are enough to achieve full, even opacity. However, for challenging colors like white, yellow, red, or any light color over a dark base, you may need a third or even a fourth thin coat to get a solid, uniform finish without any hint of the underlayer showing through.

The most important principle is that each individual coat should be thin. A thin coat means you spray from the recommended distance, typically about six to ten inches away, and you keep the can or airbrush moving so that you are depositing a mist of paint rather than a wet, pooling layer. The surface should look slightly damp but not wet, and you should still be able to see the underlying color or primer through the fresh paint. This might feel wrong because you want full coverage immediately, but trust the process. Multiple thin coats dry to a smoother, harder, and more durable finish than a single thick coat. A thick coat takes much longer to dry, is prone to drips and runs, can fill and obscure fine panel lines and surface details, and is more likely to shrink or crack as it cures.

There are some exceptions to the two to three coat rule. Metallic paints often look best with a specific approach. Many metallic paints are somewhat translucent and require a black gloss base coat to achieve their full reflective shine. Over that black base, one or two light coats of the metallic paint are usually sufficient, because applying too many coats of metallic paint can make the metallic flakes settle in a way that dulls the finish. Similarly, clear colors, such as those used for candy coat finishes, are meant to be translucent. You would apply them over a metallic base in as many thin coats as needed to achieve the desired depth of color, which could be three, four, or even five coats, each one adding richness without becoming opaque.

For hand brushing rather than spraying, the number of coats is typically higher. Hand-brushed acrylics, in particular, often require three to five very thin coats to achieve a smooth, streak-free finish because each coat is applied more thinly than a spray coat and the brush strokes need to be built up and leveled. The key with hand brushing is to let each coat dry completely before applying the next, and to thin your paint sufficiently so that it flows smoothly rather than dragging and leaving ridges.

You should also consider the final finish you want. If you are planning to apply a gloss top coat, your color coats do not need to be perfectly glossy themselves. A slightly matte or satin finish from your color coats is fine because the gloss clear coat will provide the shine. Conversely, if you are applying a matte top coat, you do not need your color coats to be perfectly smooth, as the flat finish will hide minor imperfections. However, if you are not applying any top coat, you should take extra care with your final color coat to ensure it is as even and smooth as possible.

Using airbrush

The core principle of an airbrush is based on a physical phenomenon called the venturi effect. When compressed air is forced through a narrow opening or nozzle, its velocity increases dramatically while its pressure drops. This drop in pressure creates a suction force, known as a vacuum, at the nozzle opening. That suction is what draws paint up from a reservoir, whether the reservoir is a small cup attached to the top or side of the airbrush or a bottle connected by a siphon tube. The paint is literally pulled into the stream of fast-moving air without any pumping or pushing required. Once the paint meets the high-speed air, the air tears the paint apart into millions of microscopic droplets, a process called atomization. These tiny droplets are then suspended in the air stream and carried forward onto your model. The finer the atomization, the smoother and more even the resulting paint finish will be, because the droplets are small enough to level out on the surface rather than forming visible bumps or texture.

The control you have over this process is what separates an airbrush from a simple spray can. At the heart of the airbrush is a very fine, precision-ground tapered needle that fits into a matching nozzle. When you pull back on the trigger, you retract that needle from the nozzle, opening a gap for the paint to flow through. The further you pull the trigger back, the wider the gap becomes and the more paint is released. This variable control allows you to adjust your paint flow continuously from an almost invisible wisp of paint to a broader, heavier spray, all while the air stream remains constant if your airbrush is designed for that. Many airbrushes are dual-action, meaning you press the trigger down to start the airflow and then pull it back to release paint, giving you independent control over air and paint in one smooth motion. This level of precision is impossible with spray cans, where you have very little control over the spray pattern beyond how far you hold the can from the surface.

The ability to produce such fine atomization with such precise control is why an airbrush is considered a must-have for the serious modeler, and there are several specific reasons for this. First, an airbrush can produce an incredibly smooth, flawless finish that completely lacks brush strokes. Even the most careful hand brushing leaves some texture, but an airbrushed surface can be perfectly smooth, which is essential for glossy finishes on car models or for achieving that seamless, factory-fresh look on a Gundam. Second, an airbrush allows you to apply extremely thin layers of paint. Where a spray can might deposit a coat that is many microns thick, an airbrush can be adjusted to lay down a coat that is almost transparently thin. This is crucial for preserving fine surface details like panel lines, rivets, and raised textures, because thick paint from a spray can or a brush can fill and obscure these details over time. With an airbrush, you can build up color slowly over multiple translucent coats without ever losing the sharpness of the underlying detail.

Third, an airbrush gives you unparalleled control over color blending and gradients. Because you can adjust the paint flow and air pressure independently, you can create soft transitions between colors, such as shading on a Gundam's armor panels or a realistic heat stain on a metallic thruster. You can also create highlights by spraying a lighter color from above, or shadows by spraying a darker color from below, techniques that are extremely difficult to achieve with any other painting method. Fourth, an airbrush is much more economical with paint than spray cans. A small bottle of paint, costing just a few dollars, will last for many models because the airbrush puts exactly the amount of paint you need onto the surface rather than blasting a wide, wasteful fan of paint into the air. For a serious modeler who builds multiple kits, the savings on paint alone can eventually offset the cost of the airbrush itself.

Fifth, an airbrush gives you precise control over the width of your spray pattern. With a spray can, you are generally limited to a relatively wide cone of paint, which makes it difficult to paint small or intricate parts without overspray landing on adjacent areas. With an airbrush, you can adjust the needle to produce a spray pattern as narrow as a pencil line or as wide as an inch or two, depending on your airbrush and needle size. This allows you to paint tiny details, such as a sensor camera or a thruster bell, without needing to mask off the entire surrounding area. Conversely, you can switch to a wider pattern to cover large armor panels efficiently.

There are two main types of airbrushes that serious modelers consider. A gravity-feed airbrush has a paint cup mounted on top of the body, and gravity pulls the paint down into the nozzle. These are generally preferred for fine detail work because they operate at lower air pressures and use very little paint, and the short, direct path from cup to nozzle makes them easier to clean thoroughly. A siphon-feed airbrush draws paint from a bottle mounted below or to the side using suction, and these are often preferred for painting larger models or for changing colors frequently, as you can have multiple bottles pre-filled with different colors and simply swap them. Many serious modelers own both types or choose a gravity-feed for detail work and keep a spray can or a larger spray gun for priming and clear coating large surfaces.

That said, calling an airbrush a must-have does not mean that a beginner cannot build beautiful models without one. Many excellent modelers use only spray cans and hand brushing for their entire hobby careers. However, once you reach a certain level of ambition, whether that is creating custom color blends, applying realistic shading and highlights, or achieving a flawless show-quality gloss finish, you will find that an airbrush opens up techniques that are otherwise impossible or extremely tedious. The initial investment in an airbrush and compressor can seem intimidating, but for the serious modeler who plans to build many kits over many years, it is widely considered one of the most rewarding purchases you can make. The control, the efficiency, the smoothness of finish, and the creative possibilities simply cannot be matched by any other painting tool.

Entry level airbrushes use canned gas. Advanced brushes use electric-powered air compression engine.

PS166
MR.PRO-SPRAY MK-6

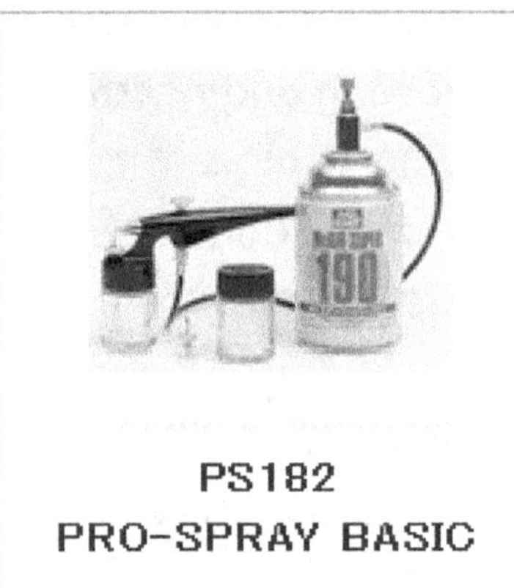

PS182
PRO-SPRAY BASIC

PS183
PRO-SPRAY DELUXE

Using spray can

For beginners, operating and maintaining an airbrush poses quite a challenge. It may be a better idea to start with spray can paint instead. Spray cans offer no flexibility since you cannot mix and match colors, however they are very easy to use and are maintenance-free.

Technically speaking, spray paint cans are nothing more than self-contained aerosol cans that utilize liquefied gases to atomize paint mixture stored inside the can. The compressed gas inside the can does not work well under cold weather. Proper room temperature must be maintained. The surface should have primer applied already. The primer must have been dried totally. The surface must be kept clean. And shake well before use. Shaking helps you create a uniformly thinned paint mixture. After shaking, remove the lid and perform a test spray to ensure the paint is coming out properly and as expected. Your can of spray paint should be at room temperature and you should shake it for 2 to 3 minutes so to mix the paint thoroughly. **ALWAYS test spray on something else first.** In fact, it is recommended that you first perform practice spraying on something else until your spraying skill is reasonably good.

When you spray paint, whether from an aerosol can or an airbrush, the goal is to deposit a thin, even layer of paint across the surface without any thick spots, runs, or dry patches. The fundamental technique to achieve this is the smooth, even pass. You start spraying before your spray pattern reaches the model, move the can or airbrush across the surface in a steady, straight line, and then release the trigger or button after you have passed beyond the edge of the model. This motion is often described as "starting off the part and ending off the part," and it prevents the heavy buildup that naturally occurs at the beginning and end of a stroke if you start and stop directly over the model. Imagine that your spray pattern is like a stripe of paint. If you start spraying directly on the model, the first moment of the spray will dump extra paint in that spot because the flow needs a split second to stabilize. Similarly, if you stop spraying while still over the model, the last bit of paint will splatter or puddle. By starting and stopping in the air beside the model, you ensure that only the steady, even middle portion of your spray stroke actually lands on the surface.

Use your entire arm rather than just your wrist is crucial for maintaining a consistent distance and angle. When you spray using only your wrist, your hand naturally arcs in a curve, which means the distance from the can tip to the model changes throughout the stroke. The can will be closest to the model at the midpoint of the arc and farther away at the ends, resulting in a heavier coat in the middle and lighter coats on the edges. This creates an uneven, striped appearance. By contrast, when you lock your wrist and move your entire arm from the shoulder, keeping your hand and the can at a fixed orientation, you can sweep the can across the model in a straight line parallel to the surface. This keeps the distance constant from the beginning to the end of the pass, which deposits a perfectly even layer of paint. It feels awkward at first, especially if you are used to writing or drawing with wrist motions, but with a little practice it becomes natural and dramatically improves your results.

The rule that a few light coats are always better than one heavy coat cannot be overstated. When you apply a single heavy coat, several problems occur simultaneously. The paint pools in panel lines and recessed details, filling them and destroying the sharpness that makes your model look realistic. The thick layer takes much longer to dry because the solvents trapped under the surface cannot evaporate easily, leading to a soft finish that remains tacky for hours or even days. As the thick paint dries, it shrinks unevenly, which can reveal sanding scratches or create a texture called orange peel, where the surface looks bumpy like the skin of an orange. Worst of all, a heavy coat can react with the plastic, especially on ABS parts, causing crazing, cracking, or a permanent hazy film. Light coats, by contrast, dry almost instantly because the thin film allows solvents to escape quickly. Each light coat builds up opacity gradually, and because the coats are thin, they level out smoothly without obscuring detail. The patience required to wait between coats is rewarded with a tougher, more uniform, and more attractive finish.

Regarding drying time, the recommendation to give several hours between coats is wise even if the paint feels dry to the touch in minutes. What you feel is the surface drying, but the lower layers of paint, especially if you are building up multiple coats, need time for solvents to fully migrate out. If you apply a second coat too soon, the solvents in the fresh paint can reactivate the still-soft first coat, causing it to lift, wrinkle, or mix unpredictably. This is particularly problematic with enamel paints, which can take twenty-four hours or more to fully cure, but even fast-drying lacquers benefit from at least thirty to sixty minutes between coats. For the final finish, many experienced modelers wait overnight before handling the model or applying clear coats.

Do note that when you keep the button or trigger depressed without moving the can, paint accumulates in one spot, and because the propellant gas continues to blast the same area, the paint can be blown into ripples or forced into a thick puddle that runs and sags. Even if you are moving the can, if you spray too slowly or linger in one area, you will get spots where the paint builds up thicker than the surrounding area, creating a mottled or blotchy appearance. The solution is to keep the can moving at a steady speed, neither too fast, which would produce a dry, dusty coat, nor too slow, which would produce runs. A speed of roughly six to twelve inches per second is a good starting point, though you will develop a feel for the right pace with practice.

A recommended spraying distance of six to eight inches, with some experts suggesting even twelve inches, serves several purposes. At close range, the propellant gas is still moving at high velocity and can literally blast the paint onto the surface, causing it to splatter or form a textured, pebbly finish. The paint also hits the surface with less time to spread out and level, so you end up with a thick, uneven layer. By holding the can farther away, the paint droplets lose some of their velocity and have time to flatten out before they land, producing a smoother finish. The distance also gives the solvents a chance to partially flash off in the air, which reduces the risk of the paint attacking the plastic or running into panel lines. That said, spraying from too far away, beyond about twelve inches, can cause the paint to dry before it hits the surface, resulting in a rough, dusty texture called dry spray. Finding the sweet spot for your particular paint and environmental conditions is something you learn with experience.

Finally, spray cans are pressurized containers with a limited shelf life, typically two to three years from manufacture under ideal storage conditions. Over time, the hydrocarbon or hydrofluorocarbon propellant gas can slowly leak past the valve seal, or the pressure can drop as the gas degrades. A can that is several years old may still spray, but the propellant may not have enough force to atomize the paint properly, resulting in sputtering, spitting, or a coarse, uneven spray pattern. The paint itself can also separate, thicken, or form solid lumps that clog the nozzle. For these reasons, it is wise to buy paint from stores with high turnover, to check the date code on the bottom of the can if one is present, and to test questionable cans on scrap plastic or cardboard before spraying your model. Storing cans upright in a cool, dry place away from direct sunlight extends their life, but even with perfect storage, a can past its prime is unlikely to perform well. When you invest time in preparing a model, it is worth using fresh, reliable paint to ensure the best possible result.

3D printing

3D printing is getting easy and cheap. An entry level 3D printer costs you less than USD$200 and there are so many free Gundam parts files available on the internet. All that you need is to download the files (most likely in .stl format), then open it up using your desktop software and set the relevant parameters.

There are a lot of tech details regarding 3D printing which is out of the scope of this book, but you are strongly encouraged to explore further! For now you want to know that this is becoming more and more affordable so it wouldn't hurt to try it out.

It is not easy to reproduce an entire model kit through 3d printing. However, producing a replacement part is technically possible and viable, and can be a real life saver!

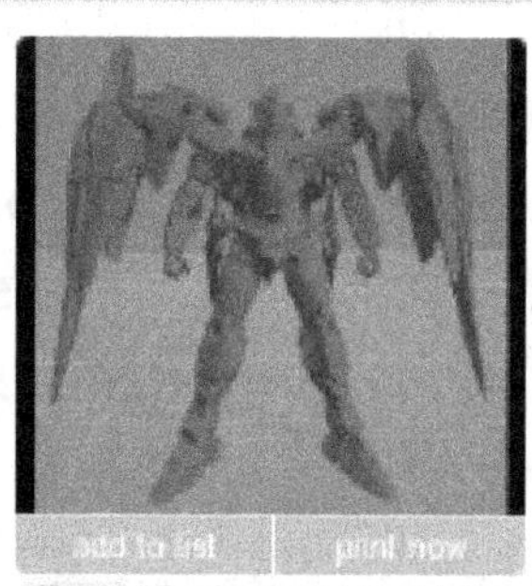

Tags 3D printable 1 144 Scale METEOR UNIT from Gundam ...

Tags 3D printer templates GN-001 Gundam Exia 3D print ...

Tags 3D print model GunDam 00 Raiser

Tags STL Gundam Logo ·

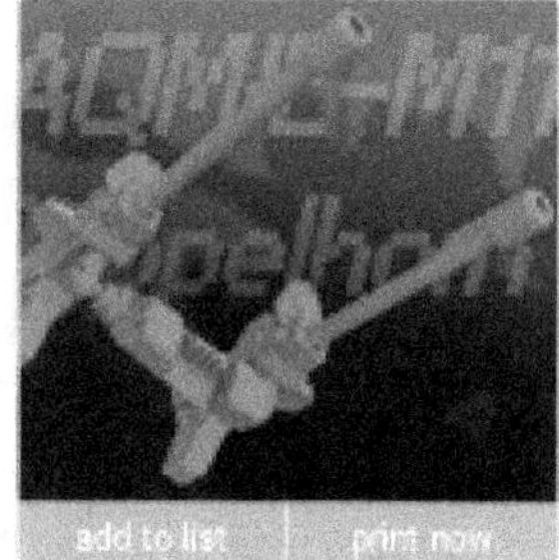

Tags [O-SD 006] AQM/E-M11 Doppelhom

Tags gundam marker airbrush adaptor

Tags [WS-002] EF-24R Flight Rotor Shrike

Tags 3D printer model Nu Gundam Beam Rifle ·

The most compelling use of 3D printing in Gunpla is for customization and scratch-building. Instead of being limited to the parts that come in a kit, you can design or download files for completely original weapons, armor plates, shoulder pauldrons, head crests, or even entire mobile suits. A notable example is God Finger, a well-known modeler who three-dimensionally printed a one-meter-tall Ultra Grade Unicorn Gundam from scratch, a project that took five months of continuous printing and resulted in a stunning, completely unique model that no store-bought kit could match. For more practical everyday use, 3D printing is excellent for creating replacement parts for broken or lost pieces, especially for older or discontinued kits that are no longer available in stores. You can also use it to produce conversion kits, where a set of three-dimensionally printed resin parts transforms an existing standard kit into a different mobile suit variant, such as the ReGelgu conversion kit for the MG

Gelgoog, which is entirely 3D printed using resin and requires assembly with superglue.

When it comes to the technology itself, you have two main paths. Desktop resin printers using SLA or DLP technology are the most popular for serious Gunpla customization because they produce incredibly high detail, capturing the fine lines and sharp edges that Gundam parts are known for. Builders using resins like Phrozen's Nylon-Green Tough Resin have successfully printed load-bearing parts such as backpacks that need to support heavy weapons. The workflow involves designing or downloading a three-dimensional model, slicing it with software, printing it, washing off uncured resin, post-curing under ultraviolet light, and then sanding and priming the part just like any other plastic kit component. The alternative is FDM printing, which uses plastic filament instead of liquid resin. FDM is cheaper and less messy, and the machines are generally more affordable and user-friendly, but the layer lines are much more visible, and achieving the smooth, sharp finish expected of Gunpla requires significantly more sanding and post-processing work. In both cases, the printed parts can be primed, painted, and top-coated exactly like standard Bandai polystyrene, so they integrate seamlessly into your existing workflow.

Thank you for reading.
For the latest content update, please visit:
http://HobbyPRESS.net/
Please email your questions and comments to editor@HobbyPRESS.net.

